MW00571681

a Vision of Peace

the Interfaith Teachings of Sri Swami Satchidananda

Rev. Sandra Kumari de Sachy, Ed.D.

Other Titles Available from Integral Yoga® Publications

Books by Sri Swami Satchidananda

Adversity and Awakening	*Kailash Journal*
Beyond Words	*The Key to Peace*
The Breath of Life	*To Know Your Self*
Free Yourself	*The Living Gita*
Gems of Wisdom	*Meditation*
The Golden Present	*Overcoming Obstacles*
The Healthy Vegetarian	*Pathways to Peace*
Heaven on Earth	*Satchidananda Sutras*
Integral Yoga Hatha	*The Yoga Sutras of Patanjali*

Books from Other Authors

Awakening: Aspiration to Realization through Integral Yoga
   by Swami Karunananda

Bound to Be Free: The Liberating Power of Prison Yoga
   by Rev. Sandra Kumari de Sachy, Ed.D.

Enlightening Tales As Told By Sri Swami Satchidananda
   edited by Swami Karunananda

Hatha Yoga for Kids by Kids by the Children of Yogaville

Inside the Yoga Sutras by Rev. Jaganath Carrera

Lotus Prayer Book edited by Swami Karunananda

Sparkling Together by Jyoti Ma

ISBN 978-1-938477-18-8

Copyright © 2014 by Satchidananda Ashram–Yogaville® Inc.
All Rights Reserved. Except as permitted under the U.S. Copyright Act of 1976, no part of this publication may be reproduced, distributed, or transmitted in any form or by any means, or stored in a database or retrieval system, without the prior written permission of the publisher or the copyright holder.

Printed in the United States of America on recycled text stock.

Integral Yoga® Publications, Satchidananda Ashram–Yogaville®, Inc.
108 Yogaville Way, Buckingham, Virginia, USA 23921
www.yogaville.org

a Vision of Peace

the Interfaith Teachings of Sri Swami Satchidananda

Rev. Sandra Kumari de Sachy, Ed.D.

Integral Yoga® Publications

Buckingham, Virginia

DEDICATION

This book is dedicated to Sri Swami Satchidananda
on the 100th anniversary of his birth.
The yogic teachings and interfaith service
of Swami Satchidananda, a beloved spiritual teacher,
have inspired and continue to inspire people
from all over the world, individuals from diverse backgrounds
and faiths who seek to experience inner peace
and to share that peace with one and all.

ACKNOWLEDGMENTS

I take this opportunity to express my heartfelt appreciation for the talented people whose generous support and effort have ensured that this project would be the joyful undertaking that it has been: Peter Petronio, our brilliant cover designer; Coleen Vimala Patterson, a talented graphic designer; Judith Prabhavati Sonntag, a superb copyeditor; Rev. Prem Anjali, a gifted production manager; Snehan de Sachy, a willing reader and perceptive critic; Swami Hamsananda, Marla Bhagavati Moffet, Karen Karuna Kreps, Becky Pushpa Ryan, our keen-eyed proofreaders.

We would also like to express our deep gratitude to Shankara Bookoff and Reverend Sivani Alderman for their generous support of the Global Garland projects in honor of the 100th Birth Anniversary of His Holiness Sri Swami Satchidananda.

In Remembrance

In remembrance of Eric Michael Margid,
beloved son, delightful friend, superb humorist,
and amazing repository of knowledge.

HINDU HYMN

Raghu Pati Raghav Raja Ram
Patit Pavan Sita Ram
Ishwar Allah tere Naam
Sabko Sanmati De Bhagwaan

King Ram! Lord of the Raghus!
Purifier of the fallen, O Sita, O Ram!
Your names are Ishwar and Allah!
Give us all your blessings, O Bhagavan!

~ A favorite of Mahatma Gandhi,
this Hindu hymn expresses the concept that God is One,
whom people call by different names.

CONTENTS

INTRODUCTION

The Visionary and the Vision

*The goal of Integral Yoga, and the birthright of every
individual, is to realize the spiritual unity behind all the
diversities in the entire creation and to live harmoniously
as members of one universal family.*

*This goal is achieved by maintaining our natural condition
of a body of optimum health and strength, senses under total
control, a mind well disciplined, clear and calm, an intellect
as sharp as a razor, a will as strong and pliable as steel, a
heart full of unconditional love and compassion, an ego as
pure as a crystal, and a life filled with Supreme Peace and Joy.*

~ Sri Swami Satchidananda

Sri Swami Satchidananda dedicated himself to serving humanity.
Tirelessly, with unconditional love and by personal example, he taught
thousands of people around the world how to use the teachings and
practices of Yoga to develop physical and emotional well-being, how
to achieve the yogic goal of living a peaceful, easeful, and useful life,
and how to experience unity in diversity.

He was a visionary who envisioned a peaceful planet, a heaven on
Earth. A guide to those who came to him seeking the way to inner
peace, he also served as a dynamic advocate for the advancement of
world peace, not in the least through his multifaceted involvement
in the interfaith movement. An interfaith pioneer, he participated
in and organized interfaith gatherings and seminars; he created
innovative interfaith programs, retreats, and worship services; and he
founded communities where people from all backgrounds and diverse
traditions could come to live and serve together. With the creation of
the Light Of Truth Universal Shrine (LOTUS), he also realized his
dream of a place where people of all backgrounds and traditions could
meditate or pray together. In that sacred temple, countless visitors have
experienced, firsthand, the principle that truth is one, paths are many.

When he arrived in the United States in 1966 as a visitor and shortly thereafter as a permanent resident, Swami Satchidananda recognized that the time had come for the East to progress materially and for the West to advance spiritually. Interacting with Western students who were eager to learn the ancient wisdom of the East, he foresaw that humanity was poised to integrate the advantages that both worlds had to offer. He also perceived that after thousands of years of human conflict—often perpetrated in the name of religion—many people, including young people, were traumatized by the pattern of senseless death and destruction that had characterized the human condition for centuries. They longed for peace, harmony, and unity.

Swami Satchidananda observed, too, that whether they identified with an established religion or whether their spiritual impulse took them on a different path, the students who sought his guidance sensed that it was time to let go of the egocentric fallacy, the delusion that we are separate, unconnected beings. They came to discover their innermost selves; they came with the sincere desire to transform themselves, to refine themselves, to grow spiritually, and, ultimately, to gain and sustain the knowledge that would lead them to experience the unity that underlies the diversity of creation.

During that time, Swami Satchidananda established a close relationship with a group of like-minded spiritual leaders that included Rabbi Joseph Gelberman, Brother David Steindl-Rast, and, later, Roshi Bernie Glassman and the Very Reverend James Parks Morton, among others. (See Appendix 1 for a full listing of these luminaries). The common thread that bound these committed peacemakers was their vision that the interfaith movement was a path to world peace. Not everyone shared their point of view. In fact, in the 1960s, a notion set forth in the previous century, most notably by the German philosopher Friedrich Nietzsche, was enjoying increased popularity in the United States. The cover of the April 8, 1966, edition of *Time* magazine asked the question "Is God Dead?" and a line of thought focused on "the death of God" was emerging in American theology. Swami Satchidananda and his interfaith colleagues understood, however, that the spiritual impulse was innately human and that religion—in one form or another—was here to stay.

One cannot deny, though, that through the ages, the religious impulse has engendered both astonishing achievements and shocking tragedies. We celebrate the magnificent cathedrals, temples, mosques, and mysterious standing stones; the art; and the enlightened teachings that inspire people all over the world. We mourn the millions who have died and grieve for those who have endured unimaginable suffering in the name of God and religion. And we offer our appreciation to those spiritual trailblazers who prove to us through the example of their own words and their own deeds that religion, no matter the name or the form, embodies a force that can be channeled to unite human beings through love rather than to divide them through hatred, as it so often has.

In this regard, *A Vision of Peace: The Interfaith Teachings of Sri Swami Satchidananda* explores the nature of religion and religious violence and how interfaith dialogue and cooperation foster and advance world peace. The book also examines the influences and experiences that shaped Swami Satchidananda's life, his teachings, his service, and his interfaith mission. Last, *A Vision of Peace* serves as a tribute to the contributions made by Swami Satchidananda as an internationally renowned Yoga master, a global peacemaker, and a modern pioneer in the increasingly expanding interfaith movement.

Though he experienced *mahasamadhi* (the act of consciously and intentionally leaving one's body at the time of death) in 2002, Sri Swami Satchidananda's life and his teachings continue to inspire and guide thousands of spiritual seekers worldwide. He will be remembered both as a revered spiritual teacher and as a key figure among those spiritual leaders whose unstinting commitment and selfless service strengthened the foundation of the dynamic, global interfaith movement that we see flourishing today.

CHAPTER 1

A Dream Come True

God leaned over me and
Whispered sweet words in my ear.
He embraced me like the sea embraces
The stream that rushes to her.
When I found myself down in the valley,
God was also there.

~ Kahlil Gibran

The peal of bells reverberated across the peaceful valley on that auspicious morning, heralding the promise of a new age of spiritual harmony. It was summer, and the temperature climbed to above 100 degrees Fahrenheit. The sun shone brilliantly. Several thousand people—men, women, and children—stood side by side, at ease in the penetrating heat. Many of them had looked forward to this moment for years, a spiritual family whose members came from all over the world. The bells rang, the traditional Indian temple horns resounded, drums beat ancient rhythms, and the heady fragrance of frankincense permeated the air. Two magnificent tigers rested peacefully on the grass. Sheltered under small canopies, they calmly observed the spectacle. Like everyone else, they, too, seemed to be anticipating a marvelous event.

Suddenly, the stirring sound of bagpipes captured everyone's attention. As the sound came closer, the crowd's gaze shifted to a nearby overlook. The bagpiper rounded the bend. Behind him, an ornately decorated baby elephant escorted a parade of colorfully costumed representatives of various faiths toward a path that led to a magnificent pink and white lotus-shaped temple. The site of the celebrants carrying blue satin banners with symbols of the world's faiths stirred hearts and souls. It was an extraordinary scene. If one had encountered such a scene in a painting, one would have thought that it was set in ancient India or Egypt or even somewhere more numinous, as one observer's experience suggested:

> When the parade first rounded the bend at the overlook and we saw the banners of the world faiths and the All Faiths banner itself, when we saw it approaching and heard the incredible sound of the bagpipes, it was an otherworldly experience. It really seemed that we had, literally, been transported to heaven. I felt it was a procession that you might see if the saints were going to come marching in.

In fact, this scene took place at the end of the 20ᵗʰ century in rural Buckingham, Virginia, U.S.A. It was here on July 20, 1986, at Satchidananda Ashram–Yogaville, that a dream became reality. This auspicious event marked the inauguration of the Light Of Truth Universal Shrine, or LOTUS, the embodiment of Sri Swami Satchidananda's vision of a world where human beings live peacefully together in the knowledge that they are all one in spirit.

As the interfaith celebrants gathered in the temple's reception building, everyone assembled under a huge tent, ready for the interfaith worship service. A hush, and then the choir began to sing "All Creatures of Our God and King" as the celebrants walked in stately procession to a stage that held an all faiths altar. The emotional impact was tremendous. Describing her personal experience, one participant also captured the experience of many:

> Seeing all the celebrants in their clerical robes—so colorful and varied—watching them march in, representing all the religions of the world, listening to the Western choir singing a traditional Western hymn, all the cultures and countries seemed to be coming together. For me, that memory said everything about what the weekend meant.

Each celebrant spoke briefly and made an offering to the central light. Then, simultaneously, they lit the one central light that symbolized the concept that there are many paths to the Divine. The ritual accorded the celebrants and congregation alike a profound experience of spiritual unity. Swami Satchidananda, or Gurudev, as his students affectionately called him, offered the following prayer:

> Beloved God in the form of this light, please accept all of our humble prayers and worship. Bless us to rise above these physical and mental limitations. Help us to experience the one Light within us all. Let us live harmoniously as Your beautiful children. Bless this holy place to vibrate peace, health, prosperity, and harmony. Let there be a lot of healing vibrations in this area so that people can be healed of all their physical, mental, and material problems.

Others also expressed their heartfelt sentiments and prayers:

Wallace Black Elk (Native American faiths): "Today, I respect this candle lighted here. This will be the light of the world. It will lighten our minds and our hearts. This was a gift to us from Grandmother, the Earth. . . . There are sacred colors, the rainbow colors. All life has sacred colors. We were a color TV world right from the beginning. Yet, so recently people discovered that. But now we're all here, and the beautiful colors are here, and we're not going to be color-blind anymore."

Rev. Victoria Parvathi Pratt-Ford (African faiths): "Let this light remain as a never-ending symbol of our constant faith that this is the truth, that we are all one, that we are all light, and that we can radiate throughout the universe with this light."

Siri Singh Sahib Yogi Bhajan (Sikhism): "Today is a special day. A united religion is born. The shrine of the LOTUS represents that unity, that grace, that divinity, and that infinity. It is that which the heart and head must bow to.

Rabbi Joseph Gelberman (Judaism): "All is one. That which seems to be an opposite really is not in opposition, because all is one."

Brother David Steindl-Rast (Christianity): "It is a great privilege to represent here the Christian tradition, not as separated but as united with all. If we address God as our father, our mother, I'm reminded of all God's children: not only the two-legged or the four-legged or the crawling ones, but all God's children."

The inspiring service came to an end. And as the choir sang Beethoven's "Ode to Joy," the celebrants walked in procession out of the tent and into the LOTUS and its upper sanctuary. Standing around the *meru* (a three-dimensional symbol representing the *axis mundi*—in religion and mythology, the world center or the connection between Heaven and Earth) in the center of the vast sanctuary, the celebrants waved lights, offered flower petals, and lit the star points of the *meru*.

At precisely 12:00 noon, the central column of light was illuminated. From floor to ceiling, it shone gloriously. Topped by a dome, the column divided into twelve rays, each ray shining down on an altar dedicated to a particular faith. Bells rang inside the shrine. Outside, hundreds of balloons were released, but a spectacular surprise was yet to come.

Each celebrant had carried a small pot of holy water from the worship service into the shrine. Inside the LOTUS, they had poured that water into one large vessel. After speeches were offered at the shrine, Gurudev took the large container of water, left the shrine with everyone following, and entered a helicopter. The fascinated crowd looked on as the helicopter lifted off and the pilot, directed by Gurudev, positioned the craft above the shrine, directly over the spire.

Many people in the crowd gasped as Gurudev leaned out of the helicopter door—placing one foot on the runner—and performed the *abishekam* (the pouring of water over a sacred object during a worship service) over the shrine. No doubt, this was a first. Loud cheers went up from the crowd as the helicopter circled the LOTUS three times. Apparently, many ideas had been offered about how to perform the *abishekam* over the shrine. But Gurudev, who loved to fly, had a clear vision from the early days of planning that the ritual would be performed from a helicopter.

From that day forward, the LOTUS was officially opened to all. The day's festivities, however, were just beginning. The afternoon was filled with musical offerings; in the evening, the LOTUS was illumined, and it glimmered like a jewel.

At the shrine, which sits alongside the LOTUS Lake, everyone gathered in a nearby tent. Each person was given a candle, and the celebrants led a procession to the lake. There they began to sing, "God's light, pure and free; Light of lights, enlighten me," and the crowd joined in.

Gurudev recited a prayer to the light. Then, they all offered their lit candles to the lake, casting them into the water. The moon was full. The stars and planets glowed. The night was crystal clear, yet lightning flashed in the distance. It was as though nature itself were making an offering to the LOTUS: a natural light show. The candles in the water began to move in a sort of pattern that drew them together; eventually, they arrived at the shore, spreading out and then aligning along the entire shore as though the event had been choreographed. What a magical, mystical day it was!

The Light Of Truth Universal Shrine symbolizes the unity that underlies the diversity of the world's faith traditions. But it also represents the selfless service, the cooperation, and the faith of the "ordinary" men, women, and children who helped to deliver this unique gift to the world: a sanctuary dedicated to spiritual harmony and world peace. As Mahatma Gandhi once said, "A small body of determined spirits fired by an unquenchable faith in their mission can alter the course of history."

The LOTUS symbolizes the human capacity to transcend the divisiveness that all too often characterizes religious experience.

All we are saying
is give peace a chance.

~ John Lennon

CHAPTER 2

The Religious Impulse, Violence, and War

Peace can never be brought by war or by force,
only by love.

~ Sri Swami Satchidananda

These days, we often hear that religious practice is declining. The British scholar and professor of theology John R. Hinnells disagrees. In his introduction to *The Penguin Handbook of the World's Living Religions* (2010), Professor Hinnells writes:

> A basic conviction behind this book is that such assertions are at most half-truths, if not wholly wrong. Perhaps formal membership of some established religious institutions is declining, but this represents only one part of the religious spectrum. In other parts religion can evidently be seen to flourish in the twentieth century: in new religious movements in primal societies in Africa or in the cities of Japan; on U.S. university campuses in the 1960s; in the powerful spirit of Islamic revivalism in the 1970s; and in the growth of "alternative" religions or charismatic movements in various continents in the 1970s and 1980s. Religion is only seen to be declining if it is viewed from a limited and "traditionalist" perspective.

In 2010, the Pew Research Center's Forum on Religion and Public Life conducted a comprehensive demographic study whose findings justify Professor Hinnells's assertion. This study of more than 230 countries estimated that there are 5.8 billion religiously affiliated adults and children around the globe, representing 84 percent of the population at that time of 6.9 billion. Thus, worldwide, more than eight out of ten people identify with a religious group. What an impressive number. It makes you wonder whether human beings are hard-wired to be religious. Indeed, some scholars believe that our religious beliefs are what make us human; in other words, they consider these beliefs to be innate rather than learned.

In "Humans Are Religious By Nature, Says Study," a piece that appeared on the online site Care2Causes (July 15, 2011), Kristina Chew discusses the findings of a group of academics who participated in an international project called "The Cognition, Religion and Theology Project" and based at England's prestigious University of Oxford. For over three years, fifty-seven researchers conducted more than forty separate studies (both empirical and analytical/interpretative) in twenty countries representing a diverse range of cultures. They found that humans are predisposed to believe in both gods and an afterlife and that "both theology and atheism are reasoned responses to what is a basic impulse of the human mind."

Chew explained that the study was undertaken not to prove that a divine power exists but, rather, to provide a better sense of whether such concepts as gods and an afterlife appear to be entirely learned or whether they are "basic expressions of human nature."

She also cites a report by *Science Daily* that describes two other findings by the Cognition, Religion and Theology Project relating to whether young children believe in some sort of "superhuman properties" and whether such beliefs reach across cultures.

In studies done by Emily Reed Burdett and Justin Barrett of the University of Oxford, children below the age of five were asked whether their mother would know the contents of a box when she couldn't see inside the box. Three-year-old children believed that their mother and God would always know the contents. By the age of four, however, children begin to understand that their mothers are not all-seeing and all-knowing. But, the study found, children may continue to believe in all-seeing, all-knowing supernatural agents, for example, a god or gods.

Whether Kristina Chew's study convinces us categorically that the God impulse is inborn—or that it is not—her statistics do illustrate that there are more people in the world who do affiliate with a religion.

Religion is, indeed, a fascinating phenomenon. Universal in scope, it is also a very personal affair. To be sure, along with politics and sex, many Americans consider it unwise to engage in discussions about religion. On the other hand, the French have a somewhat different outlook. They welcome discussions about politics and sex, but they, too, consider it inappropriate to discuss religion. In any case, while American and French conventions may differ when it comes to chatting about politics and sex, they're obviously in accord when the conversation turns to religion. Evidently, religion is a charged subject that sometimes evokes powerful reactions.

Religion. The word itself is intriguing, its etymology draped in the veils of time. The Old French term *réligion* meant piety, devotion, and religious community. Taken from the Latin word *religio*, it meant variously: respect for what is sacred; reverence for the gods; conscientiousness, sense of right, moral obligation; fear of the gods; divine service and religious observance; a religion, a faith, a mode of worship; a cult; sanctity; and holiness. In Late Latin, the term referred to monastic life. According to the Roman philosopher Cicero, the term *religio* derived from the verb *relegere*, to go through again (in reading or thought). But the popular etymology among later ancient thinkers, including Augustine, and the interpretation of many modern writers links the word to the verb *religare*, to bind fast, alluding to the bond between humans and gods, or, as the Yoga masters would phrase it, "the union of a human being's personality with his or her own divine nature." A Chan Buddhist sage, Joho, described this experience flawlessly in the following verse:

> *At last I see to the depths*
> *Of an ocean without water.*
> *No obstacles anywhere.*
> *It is all around me.*

Apart from the more mystically inclined, generally speaking, most people these days probably think of religion as a particular system of faith, of beliefs and teachings that help to explain the cosmos, human nature, and the mysteries of life.

Religions offer sacred histories, a system of morality and ethics, and a preferred lifestyle related to the recognition of and allegiance to a higher, unseen power or source. In an interview on National Public Radio, Gore Vidal, the American writer and public intellectual, once said that "art is a way to make order out of chaos." Likewise, it doesn't seem far-fetched to apply this meaning to religion. After all, despite all our modern technology and advanced scientific knowledge, the nature of the universe and human consciousness remains enigmatic and perplexing.

Religion reflects the desire of human beings to make sense of the mysteries of life and to connect with or, in the language of the mystics, to experience union with what they perceive as the source of all being, to discover the ultimate reality, and to find stability, security, and peace in a world whose only certainty is, paradoxically, uncertainty. In fact, in his book *The Belief Instinct: The Psychology of Souls, Destiny, and the Meaning of Life*, the author and psychologist Jesse Bering argues that human beings conjured up a supernatural, awe-inspiring, and protective divine being because "the illusion of a morally interested God, one that arises so naturally in our species, was a meaningful contributor to our species' success."

Undeniably, whether one considers a "morally interested God" to be an illusion created by human imagination or the ultimate reality, religion mirrors the complexities of the human psyche, reflecting the very best but also the very worst of human nature. And that's why religion—like politics, sex, and money—can be used for good purposes or for ill. As the Canadian social psychologist Ara Norenzayan says, "Religion appears to be both a maker and an unmaker of conflict." And, according to his research, religion is a phenomenon that has been, is, and will be a universal human phenomenon, perhaps *ad infinitum*.

In his book, *Big Gods: How Religion Transformed Cooperation and Conflict*, Professor Norenzayan discusses religion from the perspectives of the social sciences, the cognitive sciences, and from evolutionary biology; and he observes that "religions have always been multiplying, growing, and mutating at a brisk pace. In one estimate, new religions sprout at an average rate of two to three per day.... By one estimate, there are 10,000 religions in the world today." As the French Enlightenment philosopher and wit Voltaire put it, "*Si Dieu n'existait pas, il faudrait l'inventer*" ("If God did not exist, it would be necessary to invent him"). And in our own time, the quick-witted American political satirist Jon Stewart has observed, "Most world religions denounced war as a barbaric waste of human life. We treasured the teachings of these religions so dearly that we frequently had to wage war in order to impose them on other people."

Actually, there are many who believe that religion is in fact the cause of most wars. For example, during a sketch about the Ten Commandments, the late comedian George Carlin proclaimed: "More people have been killed in the name of God than for any other reason" (HBO Special, "Complaints and Grievances," recorded live at the Beacon Theatre in New York City, November 17, 2001). No doubt, Carlin's opinion had been influenced by the tragedy of September 11. But some years earlier—in *Back in Town*, a 1996 made-for-TV movie—Carlin declared, "If you read history, you realize that God is one of the leading causes of death."

Responding to this assertion in an article entitled "Is Religion the Cause of Most Wars?" (Huffington Post religion blog, April 10, 2012), Rabbi Alan Lurie remarked that many people share Carlin's opinion. The rabbi wrote, "When I hear someone state that religion has caused most wars, though, I will often ask the person to name these wars." The response to Rabbi Lurie's query is typically "Come on! The Crusades, the Inquisition, Northern Ireland, the Middle East, 9/11 . . ."

Like many of us, though, Rabbi Lurie wondered whether this notion was in fact correct. Apparently, it isn't, as the scholars Charles Phillips and Alan Axelrod illustrate in their definitive *Encyclopedia of Wars* (Hoboken, Wiley-Blackwell, 2012). In their list of 1,763 wars, Phillips and Axelrod classify 123 wars as having a religious cause, less than 7 percent of all wars and less than 2 percent of people killed in warfare. While these statistics belie the prevalent opinion that religion causes most wars, needless to say most people would agree that 2 percent of people killed in the name of religion is 2 percent too many.

The question that comes to mind is: Why do so many people cherish the notion that religion causes most wars? Perhaps, in light of the thousands of years of religious hostilities recorded in our history books, it's easy to jump to that conclusion if you don't take the time to investigate the details of a conflict. Once you begin to analyze the elements more closely, it usually becomes evident that these clashes are motivated by nationalism, ethnic and cultural divisiveness, political and economic issues, misconceptions, scapegoating, and the lust for power. Echoing this point of view, the anonymous author of "A Brief History of the Interfaith Movement," an essay published on the website of the Interfaith Settlement Foundation, states, "Much of the temporal interaction amongst humanity is predicated upon the pragmatic, competitive, and cooperative search for resources."

On the same topic, the cultural anthropologist Jack David Eller argues that religion is not inherently violent. An atheist himself, Eller teaches the anthropology of religion at Metropolitan State College of Denver, in Colorado. He has published a number of books on cultural anthropology and on the anthropology of religion, including *Cruel Creeds, Virtuous Violence: Religious Violence Across Culture and History*. Eller asserts that "religion and violence are clearly compatible, but they are not identical." "Violence," he maintains, "is neither essential to nor exclusive to religion, and virtually every form of religious violence has its nonreligious corollary."

In any case, while religion itself may not be the cause of most wars, it is the cause of some wars. There's no doubt about that. Clearly, religious violence impedes global peace, well-being, and harmony. Recorded history confirms that violence generated in the name of God and religion has brought immeasurable suffering and destruction to Earth's inhabitants and to the planet itself. Centuries ago, it was the Crusades in Europe and the Middle East; the wars between Catholics and Protestants in France and other European nations; the Inquisition in Spain, where thousands of Jews were either forced to convert or murdered and sometimes both.

The 19th and 20th centuries suffered their share of religious violence: the pogroms that slaughtered thousands of Jews in Eastern Europe and the holocaust of World War II, where millions of Jews and people of other faiths were tortured and killed because of their religion, as well as their political affiliations, physical and mental conditions, and sexual orientation. In more recent times: the Buddhist attacks on

Muslims in Myanmar, the violence between Buddhists and Hindus in Sri Lanka, and the events of September 11, 2001, in the United States.

Sadly, current headlines continue to flood our consciousness with examples of religious intolerance. Christians and Muslims are fighting one another in Nigeria and the Central African Republic, Sunnis and Shias are killing one another in Iraq, Afghanistan, and other countries, Jews and Muslims are committing violence against one another in Israel and Palestine, and so on and so on.

Writing about interfaith dialogue in an essay for the online resource site Oxford Islamic Studies Online, the American professor Natana J. Delong-Bas points out that, historically, many religions have tended to view other religions as holding incorrect beliefs, committing heresy, apostasy, and blasphemy, and generally as being unequal to their own. Monotheistic religions particularly viewed their tradition as possessing the one and only truth. And although early interfaith encounters occurred, they tended to adopt the format of religious competitions, where each religion set out to explain why it was superior to the others rather than listening to what the members of the other traditions had to say.

Throughout history, though, there have been leaders who have attempted to understand and engage, as Delong-Bas put it, "the religious other." For example, ancient leaders who practiced religious tolerance included Cyrus the Great (669–530 BCE) and Darius the Great (550–486 BCE) of Persia; King Asoka of India (273–232 BCE); Emir Abd-ar-Rahman III of Al Andalus (912–961 CE); and Kublai Khan, grandson of Genghis Kahn, of the Mongol Empire (1215–294 CE).

Fortunately, in more recent times, meetings between members of different faith traditions have shifted to structures where participants explain their own perspectives nonconfrontationally and listen actively and respectfully to the viewpoints of others. Today, participants in interfaith gatherings focus not only on theological similarities and differences but also on mutual awareness, understanding, respect, and acceptance.

In her essay, Delong-Bas maintains that the impetus for this alternative approach to interfaith encounters is twofold. She explains that, first, beginning in the late 19ᵗʰ century, a series of missionary and faith conferences—Christian-Hindu meetings in India, for instance—helped to promote interest in formal theological discussions with individuals from other religions. Second, she cites globalization, with its accompanying advances in transportation and communication technology, as another reason for the increase in interfaith meetings on the informal level, along with the extensive migration of people and ideas. People began to have more access to diverse knowledge systems, as well as more exposure to the customs, traditions, and languages of people from other cultures.

In the 1950s, all those factors coalesced into an interfaith dialogue movement. In the West, the World Council of Churches (Protestant) and the Vatican (Roman Catholic) organized a series of meetings between Christian leaders and representatives from other religions. Those meetings culminated in the creation of the Secretariat for Non-Christian Religions (later renamed the Pontifical Council for Interreligious Dialogue) at the Vatican to study religious traditions, to provide resources, and to promote interreligious dialogue through education and the facilitation of local efforts by Roman Catholics. In January 1959, Pope John XXIII (now Saint John XXIII) called the Second Vatican Ecumenical Council, popularly known as Vatican II. Many people were quite surprised, as this would be the first ecumenical council held in nearly a hundred years.

Vatican II took place from 1962 to 1965, producing several major documents on interfaith relations, documents that encouraged friendship with other faiths. Among the reforms put forth by the new council was reconciliation with the Jewish community, including the church's rejection of persecution (of any person), hatred, and displays of anti-Semitism directed against Jews at any time and by anyone. According to Sr. Maureen Sullivan, who authored two books on Vatican II (*101 Questions and Answers on Vatican II and The Road to Vatican II: Key Changes in Theology*), Pope John often said that it was time to open the window of the church to let in some fresh air.

Meanwhile, during the same time period that Pope John XXIII was advancing interfaith cooperation through the reforms of Vatican II in Italy, Sri Swami Satchidananda—then director of the Divine Life Society branch in Ceylon—was also fostering interfaith harmony through his welcoming response to *ashram* (spiritual community) visitors from different faiths, as well as through his innovative interfaith celebrations.

On reflection, the simultaneity of these two events—one occurring in the East and one in the West—evokes the familiar opening and closing verse of a poem that Rudyard Kipling wrote in 1889, *The Ballad of East and West*:

> Oh, East is East, and West is West,
> and never the twain shall meet,
> Till Earth and Sky stand presently
> at God's great Judgment Seat;
> But there is neither East nor West,
> Border, nor Breed, nor Birth,
> When two strong men stand face to face,
> tho' they come from the ends of the earth!

The strength of such individuals, both men and women, reflects the character of those whose thoughts and actions are motivated by the union of empathy and equanimity, the unity of heart and head. To quote one of Swami Satchidananda's witticisms:

> *If you always use your head to decide everything, you will always find differences, because egoism resides in the head. That's why you never hear of "sweetheads." But when people come together in the heart, they are real sweethearts. A totally headless heart is too emotional, but let the heart be there first. Then, in God's name, come together and enjoy that relationship.*

CHAPTER 3

Mystics, Sages, and Saints

I searched for God and found only myself.
I searched for myself and found only God.

~ Sufi proverb

Sri Swami Satchidananda was born in 1914 in Chettipalayam, a small village in Tamil Nadu, South India. Ramaswamy, or Ramu, as he was called then, was the son of a landowning family, landlords who didn't work the land but who supervised the *dalits*, the laborers traditionally known as "untouchables." As the scion of a family that owned hundreds of acres, Ramu was not permitted to do farm work, which was considered menial. But, even from a very early age, Ramu took a different, independent and iconoclastic turn, in his perspective as well as his behavior. "Listen," he whispered to the wary farm workers. "No one is watching. They'll never know if I do it." Secretly, he was permitted to use the farm tools, and some days he would even sneak off to the *dalit* colony.

From his very childhood, Ramu was inclined to treat everyone with respect, no matter the caste or the station in life, and, later on, no matter the ethnicity, the religion, or the beliefs. He ignored the cultural conventions and customs that he saw to be inequitable and unjust. Instead, even as a child, he had an innate understanding of the essential principles and teachings of the ancient spiritual tradition into which he was born. In the West, we refer to that tradition as Hinduism (the word "Hindu" is derived from the Persian term for the Sanskrit word "Sindu," the historic local name for the Indus River). In India, they call it *Sanatana Dharma. Sanatana*, in the ancient Indian language Sanskrit, means eternal, never ending. The term *Dharma* derives from the root verb *dhr*, to hold, to keep, to maintain. *Dharma* is also translated as "the law" and "the way." In English *Sanatana Dharma* is often defined as the eternal way or, as the British author and critic Aldous Huxley put it, the perennial philosophy.

Sanatana Dharma, or Hinduism, is actually a family of religions that consists of many diverse traditions; it has no single founder or prophet and goes beyond any historical founding date. It is based on experience rather than belief. And Ramu's character, his attitude, and his actions exemplified the qualities of compassion, morality, wisdom, and pure insight embodied in the teachings of the *Sanatana Dharma*, characteristics that emanate naturally from one who is in tune with the harmony of universal law.

Eventually, Ramu's interests, aptitudes, and destiny led him to the university and to the study of agricultural engineering, to the cinematography and automotive fields, to temple management, to the householder life, and, finally, to the life of a renunciate.

In 1945, after a year of seclusion, introspection, and meditation in a hut on his family's land, he set out to experience the next stage of his spiritual journey, heading for the sacred Palani Hill and the *ashram* of the family Guru, Sadhu Swamigal. Sadhu Swamigal was a great *upasika*, or *tantric* yogi, who used geometrical forms, or *yantras*, as well as certain mantras (sacred sounds), *mudras* (symbolic hand gestures), and cleansing practices during the course of worship to invoke the presence of a particular deity. (Ultimately, the *upasika* receives that presence or vision within.) Ramu also visited the Sri Sai Baba Center in Coimbatore, where he assisted with organizational matters.

South India was full of *siddhas*, yogis who were believed to have supernatural powers, and many of them traveled from place to place incognito, never publicly demonstrating their abilities. Some of them appeared to be wanderers, vagabonds, and even madmen. One such *siddha* was known by all as Paper Baba, so called because, although he was illiterate, he always carried a rolled newspaper under his arm; he also held a stick in his hand. No one knew how old Paper Baba was, but he had been seen in the area for many years. Paper Baba never allowed anyone to live with him as a disciple, but whenever he came across sincere spiritual seekers, he would give them some advice and then send them off with a blessing.

When Ramu found him walking cautiously along a road, Paper Baba appeared to be blind, feeling the way with his stick, a rolled-up newspaper tucked tightly in his armpit. When Ramu crept up silently behind him, though, Paper Baba whirled around and, with one swift motion, demanded, "Who are you, and why are you following me?"

Surprised, Ramu composed himself and explained that he was a humble seeker who had come for a blessing. But Paper Baba retorted, "Who blesses whom? Go! Go away!"

What puzzled Ramu was how the blind *sadhu* (wandering mendicant) knew that he was being followed. Even more surprising was that Paper Baba not only refused to give his blessings but, lifting his arm above his head, threatened to hit Ramu with his stick. To Ramu that gesture alone would have been a blessing, and he told the *sadhu* that. Seeing how tenacious Ramu was, Paper Baba relented and blessed him with the gift of a basket of limes to enjoy and to share with others. When Ramu began giving away all the limes, Paper Baba stopped him and told him to keep some for himself. Then, he shouted at Ramu to get out and to stop running after him but not before whispering in Ramu's ear, "Everything will be all right."

During his stay at Sadhu Swamigal's *ashram*, Ramu lived in complete seclusion for fifty-one days, rigorously practicing Yoga and meditation. After a while, without his making any conscious effort to attract them, many pilgrims coming to the area began visiting him for instruction, and a large number of them came to him for healing. For those people, Ramu kept a coconut shell container filled with holy ash outside the hut. When people told him about the particular condition that they or their loved ones were suffering, he would advise them to take a little bit of the ash and put it on the area that needed healing.

One night, a local man whose wife had been in labor for ten hours and was in great pain came to the hut. He asked Ramu to bless his wife with an easy delivery. Ramu gave him some of the holy ash and told him to mix it with a little water and to give it to the woman to drink. The smooth delivery took place almost immediately after she drank the water. Invariably, all of Ramu's cures occurred just as he predicted. During his *sadhana* (spiritual practice), he had prayed for such a power, and he had received it. In fact, he would often close his eyes and pray, "God, please bless me so that I might cure the pains of others."

After a time, however, Ramu began to feel dissatisfaction with his methods. Somehow, as he described it, he felt that something wasn't right. He remembered learning that one should not interfere with "God's work." Perhaps because the ego was involved, the result would be that he would lose all the peace he had gained through his spiritual practices. At that point, he stopped asking for curative powers, thinking to himself, "Who am I to take other people's karma [the total effect of one's actions, during all lifetimes, that determines one's fate], that is, karma that they needed to experience themselves?" From then on, when people came to him for cures, he would recommend certain changes in their diet or special breathing techniques and other practices, so that they themselves could take an active part in their own healing and not depend on Ramu's effort alone. In that way, they could purge their karma and not be bound by any reaction.

While Ramu was in Palani, he had the opportunity to study with a number of great *siddhas*. One of Ramu's friends was a devotee of Sri Swami Jnanananda Giri. One day, his friend took Ramu to have the *darshan* (the occasion to see or be in the presence of a holy person) of that reputedly 160-year-old *siddha*. The swami graciously received Ramu, and they had lunch together. During the meal, the ancient swami questioned Ramu, referring to certain matters in which Ramu was involved. Swami Jnanananda Giri seemed to have prior knowledge of Ramu's activities, although they had never met before. In fact, as they spoke, the swami predicted that Ramu would leave India. "This is not the only place for you," he told him. "You should travel. Many of these people don't appreciate anything. They only want *siddhis*." Ramu replied straightforwardly and with conviction, "Swamiji, if you feel that way, then let it happen."

After having photographs taken with Ramu, Swami Jnanananda Giri sent one of the devotees to the shrine room to fetch a beautiful sandalwood fan. He presented the lovely object to Ramu, who opened it and proceeded to fan the great *siddha*. As he fanned the swami, one of the devotees told Ramu in a whisper that the fan was a precious gift offered to Swami Jnanananda Giri with much love and devotion by one of his students and that the swami must be "really happy" with Ramu to have given him such a gift.

Hearing this, Ramu felt that he shouldn't accept the swami's gift. It seemed to him that the devotee who offered the fan might feel hurt that the swami had given it away. So, when the time came for him to leave, Ramu unobtrusively—he thought—left the fan behind. He got into the car, the driver started the engine, and they began to drive away. Suddenly, the car stopped dead in its tracks, and the driver couldn't restart it. As he tried in vain to start the car, Swami Jnanananda Giri came running out of the *ashram* with the fan. Apparently, his advanced age didn't deter him. Reprimanding Ramu, he admonished him for not taking the gift with him.

Ramu apologized, explaining that he'd forgotten it. However, he couldn't pull the wool over this swami's eyes, which twinkled as he let Ramu know that he wasn't fooled. "Come on," he shouted, "take it!" The minute that Ramu took the fan, the car started. These were but two of the great *siddhas* around Palani from whom Ramu learned many important lessons that influenced his life and his teachings.

In 1946, Ramu devised a spiritual experiment. He decided to wander throughout South India as a mendicant, keeping in mind this thought: "If there is a God, then He will take care of me." As part of this test, he took two vows: not to keep any money and not to ask anyone for anything, including food.

For four months, he wandered wherever his feet took him. During the first three days, he had nothing to eat. Eventually, a young man approached him, asking him whether he'd eaten, as he looked hungry. When Ramu replied that he hadn't eaten in three days, the man quickly brought him a meal. When Ramu felt tired, he would simply lie down wherever he found himself and go to sleep—sometimes by the side of a road, sometimes on a park bench. He never remained in one area for more than three days, and he often visited temples, where he was allowed to sleep on the big verandas and bathe in the ponds. After the morning worship, the temple priests would distribute food, but Ramu adhered strictly to his vow and never stood in the food line. He would eat only if someone noticed him sitting off to the side and brought him a plate of food.

Sometimes, he walked; other times, he took advantage of rides that were offered, even traveling by train, because in those days the railroads provided free travel for *sadhus*. A *sadhu* would go to the station and simply sit on a bench patiently until a railway attendant noticed him and asked his destination. The railway personnel considered it a great blessing to take personal charge of a *sadhu*. In fact, the conductor would make sure that the *sadhu* had a nice seat and something to eat and drink, and every so often he would inquire after the holy man's comfort. In fact, if the conductors were changed, the first conductor would introduce his replacement, and the new conductor would continue respectfully caring for the *sadhu*.

By and by, Ramu felt a pull drawing him north toward the Himalayas. And in 1947, while he was in Calcutta, he decided to journey to Rishikesh, in the Himalayan foothills. Rishikesh has for centuries been the abode of many sages and saints, some living in caves, some living in huts, and some living in *ashrams* near the holy Ganges River. Ramu had heard about the illustrious sage Sri Swami Sivanandaji Maharaj, who had an *ashram* on the banks of the Ganges. He felt a profound wish to have the *darshan* of this holy being.

Ramu sat on a bench at the Calcutta railway station, waiting patiently for an attendant to ask his destination; half the day passed without any train official noticing him. However, others did take notice, and soon many people gathered around him, bringing food for him to bless and to distribute as *prasad* (devotional offering) and sitting around him as he gave *satsang* (spiritual discourse). Finally, a conductor arrived to escort him to a train. But because of an outbreak of political riots plaguing the country at the time, all passages heading north were blocked, and Ramu had to postpone his Himalayan trip. Instead, he traveled to Pondicherry in order to have the *darshan* of the great yogi and brilliant scholar Sri Aurobindo.

Sri Aurobindo Ghose was a poet, philosopher, and educator. He was often seen as politically controversial, because he spoke out vociferously about Indian independence from Great Britain. But behind Sri Aurobindo's outspokenness dwelt a deeply spiritual vision of India held by a patriot who believed that his country should be ruled by *Sanatana Dharma*, the Eternal Law. Although Aurobindo Ashram grew up around this great yogi whose spiritual experiences had completely transformed his life, Sri Aurobindo spent most of his time in seclusion, performing Yoga *sadhana*. He gave *darshan* only four times a year, but through his prolific writing he presented detailed instructions to his students.

Ramu received the blessings of this great master and his foremost disciple, the Mother, and then continued his journey through South India as a wandering mendicant. He frequently visited Ananda Ashram to spend time with Papa Ramdas and Mother Krishnabai and spent considerable time at the Ramakrishna Mission. There he received pre-*sannyas* initiation (pre-monastic rites) from Swami Chidbhavananda, who gave him his new pre-*sannyas* name, Sambasivam Chaitanya.

Sri Ramakrishna, spiritual founder of the Sri Ramakrishna Movement, was a 19th-century mystic from India. He was a Hindu, but, without repudiating Hinduism, he also practiced other religions, notably Islam and Christianity. When he practiced those religions, he surrendered to them completely. In 1866, for example, Sri Ramakrishna gave himself totally to Islam, repeating the name of Allah, wearing traditional Muslim clothing, and eating the traditional foods that Muslims ate. In fact, his self-surrender to the Islamic way resulted in his direct experience of the Divine, just as it did when he followed his Hindu path. Seven years later, he proved empirically that one could experience the same truth on the Christian path. For a time, he became completely absorbed in the idea of Christ, focusing solely on those thoughts.

According to Ananda K. Coomaraswamy, in a lecture given in March 1936 for the centenary celebration of Sri Ramakrishna's birth, one might have supposed that Sri Ramakrishna had converted to Christianity. But he clarified what had really occurred: "I have also practiced all religions, Hinduism, Islam, Christianity, and I have also followed the paths of different Hindu sects.… The lake has many shores. At one, the Hindu draws water in a pitcher and calls it *jala*;

at another the Muslim [collects water] in leather bottles and calls it *pani*; and at a third, the Christian [collects] what he calls water." (The foregoing was taken from a lecture originally given in New York, in March 1936, for the centenary of the birth of Sri Ramakrishna.)

Such an understanding may be rare, states Coomeraswamy; but, he insists, it is normal in the East. To support that assertion, Coomeraswamy quotes Lord Krishna in the Hindu scripture, the *Bhagavad Gita*: "There is no deity that I am not, and in case any man be truly the worshiper of any deity whatever, it is I that am the cause of his devotion and its fruit. . . . However men approach Me, even so do I welcome them, for the path men take from every side is Mine."

Undoubtedly, during his extended stay at the Ramakrishna Mission, Sambasivam was exposed to the unique interfaith perspective of Sri Ramakrishna and to the teachings of Swami Vivekananda, one of Ramakrishna's chief disciples. As a young man in 1893, Swami Vivekananda made his way from India to America to represent Hinduism at the first Parliament of the World's Religions in Chicago.

Sambasivam left the Ramakrishna Mission in 1946 to continue his spiritual journey, and before reaching Rishikesh, he studied and served with various other sages, including the great Jnana Yogi Sri Ramana Maharshi. A *jivanmukta*, or living liberated being, Sri Ramana's teaching was based on seeking the answer to the eternal question, "Who am I?" His method was grounded in the Indian philosophical system known as *Advaita*, or Nondualism. The fundamental teaching of *Advaita* is that there is only one supreme reality, which is called *Brahman*. *Brahman*, the Supreme Being, is infinite and omnipresent. Nothing can be added to *Brahman*, and there's no place where *Brahman* doesn't exist. *Brahman* is nondual. The world and everything associated with it, including human beings, do not exist outside of *Brahman*.

From this perspective, the world itself is unreal, an illusion. To draw an analogy, the world is equivalent to a dream that has its own, subjective reality but is illusory compared to the waking state. Further, because of *avidya*, or spiritual ignorance, we have forgotten our true nature and mistakenly believe that we are limited individuals, separate from everyone and everything. However, there is a solution to this dilemma: Jnana Yoga, which is the practical application of *Advaita*.

Jnana Yoga, the Yoga of knowledge or wisdom, is the direct path, through self-inquiry, to experiencing the truth of *Advaita*, that is, the realization of the true Self as the *Atma*, the essence that is eternal, unchanging, and indistinguishable from the essence of the universe. *Brahman* is beyond description. The ancient *rishis* (sages or seers) taught—based on their personal experience—that this experience can best be described as *sat-chit-ananda*. *Sat* means pure, absolute existence, being or truth. *Chit* means pure, absolute knowledge and consciousness. And *Ananda* means pure, absolute bliss. Our true nature, then, is pure existence, knowledge, and bliss.

Finally, Sambasivam's sometimes challenging, often adventurous, and always steadfast pilgrimage led him to his goal. He arrived in Rishikesh in May 1949, finding his way to Sivananda Ashram, the headquarters of the Divine Life Society. There he met his Guru, Sri Swami Sivananda. Two months later, in July, Swami Sivananda initiated him into the Holy Order of *Sannyas* (initiation into a life of renunciation and selfless service) and gave him a new spiritual name: Swami ("one who is master of oneself") Satchidananda (Truth-Knowledge-Bliss). With a new name and a new role, Swami Satchidananda, Gurudev, moved closer to fulfilling his destiny.

While living at Sivananda Ashram, Gurudev often visited Vashishta Guha (Vashishta's Cave), several miles away. Vashishta was a great *rishi*, or sage, who lived hundreds of years ago. Legend has it that it was in this cave that he engaged in ascetic practices. When Gurudev began going there, a saintly contemporary of Swami Sivananda's named Swami Purushottamanandaji Maharaj lived there. It was a perfect spot for meditation, and Gurudev became quite close to the saint. The two would sit and talk outside on a platform, and, after the inspiring *satsang* (being in the company of the highest truth or sitting with a guru), the young *sannyasin* would ask for permission to go inside to meditate. It was here, in September 1949, that he experienced the following:

My highest experience, which was not connected with any particular form, was the experience of *Advaita* or Oneness. I had that in 1949, a few months after my *sannyas* initiation. It was in midwinter when I visited Vashishta Cave. . . . I went into the cave, bending down, until, after twenty-five feet, I reached a large room-like place with a seat. As I sat there and meditated, I had the experience of transcending my body and mind, realizing myself as the Omnipresent. I forgot my individuality. It is impossible to explain exactly what this is.

I must have spent several hours in that state. Then, I heard a humming sound, *OM* chanting, coming from a long distance away. Slowly, slowly, it became louder. As it neared, I became aware of my mind and body. Gently, I stood up and went out of the cave.

For some time, I couldn't see anything in the normal way. All over, I saw light, light, light. The whole world appeared to be a mass of light. There was only peace everywhere. The state persisted that whole day.

After that, I had this experience very often, mostly when I visited a holy place. I had it in Badrinath and almost every day when I went to Mount Kailash. I had it in Amarnath in Kashmir. Even in Sri Lanka, whenever I visited Adam's Peak. I had it in Jerusalem and in St. Peter's in Rome.

~ from *Sri Swami Satchidananda* (a biography)

In a little more than a decade, Gurudev's destiny would take him all over the world. Based in the United States, he would inspire thousands—through his teachings, his selfless service, and his own life—to lead healthier and happier lives. He touched hearts and opened minds with his message that all faiths lead to the truth and that, ultimately, each one of us will experience that truth. Enlightenment, or what some call Cosmic Consciousness, Self-realization, or God-realization, he declared, was everyone's birthright and everyone's fate.

CHAPTER 4

All Paths Lead Home

In God's eyes the man stands high who makes peace between men.
But he stands highest who establishes peace among the nations.

~ Pirkei Avot (*Ethics of the Fathers*, 1:18), Jewish Scripture

It was at Sivananda Ashram that Gurudev's interfaith awareness expanded as he observed his beloved spiritual master welcoming disciples who held widely divergent beliefs and views. In fact, Swami Sivananda did more than welcome these seekers. He loved, appreciated, and respected them all. As Swami Sivananda saw it, "All religions are one, all religions are equally valid, equally great, equally sharers of truth." He even welcomed religious fanatics, never offending or provoking them, but rather dealing with them from the heart, at the human level. In his view, it was possible that each religion represented a partial view of the truth. He likened the situation to looking out the window at the sky. When we look at the sky, can any of us see the whole sky? No. Each one of us sees only a portion of the whole.

In 1953, Swami Sivananda organized a Parliament of Religions, inviting a number of scholars who belonged to different faiths. A monist, he believed that there is only One and that what we call God is not in a statue or in a temple. That is to say, God is not confined to a particular form. Yet, Swami Sivananda never criticized people who worshipped God in those places or in the form of a statue. In fact, if someone came to the *ashram* and mentioned that he worshipped God in a particular form, Swami Sivananda acknowledged that and encouraged the person to build a small shrine for the image and to worship it there. On the other hand, if someone came along who didn't believe in that way of worshipping or in any way of worshipping for that matter, Swami Sivananda never argued. To him, God was omnipresent, God was everywhere. Then why did he encourage people to worship God in a temple, in a church, in a synagogue? Why didn't he insist that they worship God everywhere? Because he knew that these people's perspectives reflected their limited vision and that they would come to maturity in their own time.

Swami Sivananda was eager to listen to everyone, encouraging them all to pursue their own path, to embrace their own philosophy of life. They needn't abandon their religion, their method of worship and meditation, their way of life. What's more, he encouraged his devotees to study others' points of view—they might have something interesting to say—and to develop friendliness, affection, and understanding. One of his sayings was: "Break down the barriers that separate man from man." According to Swami Venkatesananda, one of his secretaries, "He repeated this hundreds of times, whenever he spoke . . ." "Realize that you are a human being," he instructed. "What your religion may be is your personal affair." And his "Universal Prayer," which is repeated daily at Satchidananda Ashram–Yogaville, expresses his all-embracing vision of the Cosmic One:

> O adorable Lord of mercy and love!
> Salutations and prostrations unto Thee.
> Thou art omnipresent, omnipotent, and omniscient.
> Thou art *Sat-Chid-Ananda* [Existence-Knowledge-Bliss Absolute].
> Thou art the Indweller of all beings.
>
> Grant us an understanding heart,
> equal vision, balanced mind,
> faith, devotion, and wisdom.
> Grant us inner spiritual strength
> to resist temptation and to control the mind.
> Free us from egoism, lust, anger, greed, hatred and jealousy.
> Fill our hearts with divine virtues.
>
> Let us behold Thee in all these names and forms.
> Let us serve Thee in all these names and forms.
> Let us ever remember Thee.
> Let us ever sing Thy glories.
> Let Thy name be ever on our lips.
> Let us abide in Thee for ever and ever.

In the same year that he organized the Parliament of Religions in Rishikesh, Swami Sivananda met with a disciple who was also called Swami Satchidananda. This Swami Satchidananda was a woman who belonged to the Tamil-speaking community in Ceylon, and devotees there wanted to open a branch of the Divine Life Society. Swami Sivananda thought it would be a good idea to open a branch with an orphanage attached to it. And because they spoke the same language, the two Satchidanandas often sat and talked, so it wasn't surprising that the female Satchidananda requested that her brother monk join her in starting the new branch and the orphanage on land owned by her family. The male Satchidananda, however, was perfectly content to remain at the *ashram*, teaching Yoga philosophy and Hatha Yoga at the Vedanta Forest Academy *ashram* school; and he wanted nothing more than to continue his meditation in seclusion. Although the other Satchidananda already knew of his reluctance, she chose him because he was an excellent teacher and also because he spoke Tamil.

Swami Sivananda approved wholeheartedly. However, when he approached his reluctant disciple, the *sannyasin* insisted that he wasn't fit to do such work and that there were probably other devotees who would like to go to Ceylon. As for him, he'd be content to stay in Rishikesh and continue his service there. Determined, Gurudev thought that his refusal would put an end to the issue. But Swami Sivananda had other plans. "Don't worry," he said. "I will work through you."

Undeterred, Gurudev tried another approach. "Swamiji, we are both called Swami Satchidananda. How will people differentiate between the two Satchidanandas? What will happen when we receive mail? There will be confusion. Certainly, there will be confusion."

Swami Sivananda just laughed. He had the perfect solution: "From now on, she will be known as Swami Satchidananda Mataji [*mataji* means mother], and you can use *Yogiraj*—the title I gave you [*Yogiraj* means Yoga master]." Thus, the matter was settled, and Gurudev and Mataji left their master in Rishikesh at the close of 1952. They arrived in Ceylon in February of 1953. And after visiting all the fields owned by Mataji's family, the two swamis selected ten acres near Trincomalee on which to build the *ashram*.

The next phase of Gurudev's life had begun. Never again would he find much time for seclusion. Although he himself had no desire for recognition or for disciples, more and more people began to see him as their beloved spiritual teacher, their guide, their Guru.

Construction of the *ashram* was completed in September, and while the *ashram* was being built, Gurudev lodged in a nearby boardinghouse, holding talks and teaching Hatha Yoga at the Hindu College, run by the Ramakrishna Mission. One day, someone asked Gurudev why, as a swami from the Divine Life Society, he was giving classes and talks at the Ramakrishna Mission School. Gurudev replied, "What is the difference? The Ramakrishna Mission is also Divine Life. Every spiritual institution is a Divine Life institution. They have different names, but there is no real difference." Gurudev's response embodies the wisdom that was to inform his teachings, his service, and his life: though names and forms may differ, their essence is the same. As the ancient Indian scripture the *Rig Veda* states: "Truth is one; the wise call it by many names."

Mrs. Rukmini Rasiah, who served as head of the Jaffna, Ceylon, *ashram* and director of its Fine Arts Society, said of Gurudev:

> The rich, the poor, people from all walks of life, of all castes and creeds, of all ages, were treated alike by him. The farmers and the government agents all had to sit together. Only the little children received special treatment. He was a friend to all.... The religion he taught was the simple precepts of his great master. "Serve and love" was taught first, and he practiced what he taught ...
>
> Priests of all denominations came to the *ashram*, and Gurudev gave them clarification of their own religions.
> He did not believe in converting anyone ...
>
> ~ from *Sri Swami Satchidananda*

Mrs. Rasiah once confided that during his tenure in Ceylon, Gurudev was dubbed "the controversial swami" because he wore a watch, drove a car, taught classes, and served everyone—not just Hindus, but people from all different faiths. He never tried to draw anyone away from his or her own faith. Rather, he spoke to them through the teachings of their own tradition, because he was well versed in the scriptures and principles of other religions, Eastern and Western. He wasn't reclusive like many of the swamis. He was a swami of the people. In this regard, he was also a reformer, advocating for their rights and speaking out against the mistreatment of the poor, so-called coolies who worked the land of the big estates that dotted the area.

In July of 1953, the Ceylon Divine Life Society devotees were getting ready to celebrate Guru Poornima Day. This festival is held on the full moon day in the month of July, and it's a day set aside for special worship of the guru, including talks on his or her life. The devotees began collecting pictures of Swami Sivananda and setting them up around the *ashram*. Observing them, Gurudev thought for a while about what the disciples were doing, and then he spoke to them about what was on his mind. He reminded them that people from all different religions were coming to the *ashram* to see him and that he had invited them to this celebration. How would they feel, he asked, if all they saw around them were pictures of Swami Sivanandaji? They might feel that their own teachers had been left out. After all, he continued, this is supposed to be a day dedicated to focusing on the guru, and there are many gurus for all the different people.

So, the disciples set about collecting pictures of masters from all religions, covering the walls with images of Jesus, Buddha, Sri Aurobindo, Ramakrishna Paramahansa, Ramana Maharshi, Siva, Vishnu, and many others. The day was proclaimed as "All Prophets Day," and it became an annual event where the various leaders of Ceylon's different religious factions came together to discourse on the truths behind the particular religions. As the chairman, Gurudev reiterated the message embodied in the celebration, the universal truth that he had always believed in and that his own master had taught and lived by: "Truth is one; paths are many." This, the first All Prophets Day in Ceylon in 1953, marked the formal beginning of Gurudev's interfaith service and a mission that was to continue for another half a century.

Informally, Gurudev fostered religious harmony through his everyday encounters. For instance, he felt a natural affinity with followers of the Bahá'í faith, whose founder, Bahá'u'lláh, emphasized the spiritual unity of all humanity, and they were drawn to him. Wherever he traveled, if there was a Bahá'í temple nearby, he would visit it. Also, whenever he was in the area, he would stop by the shop of a devout young Muslim man who liked Gurudev's teachings so much that he would come to the *ashram* to practice various aspects of Yoga.

Gurudev became well acquainted with the man's entire family, but he was still surprised when the shopkeeper asked him whether he could send his niece to stay at the *ashram* for a while in the hope that the Yoga practices would help cure her asthma. Of course, Gurudev would welcome the girl to the *ashram*, but he was also sensitive to the Islamic customs, and he asked whether the girl herself wanted to go to the *ashram* and whether the family agreed with the plan. The man assured Gurudev that they all had complete confidence and trust in him and that they felt as though the girl were his own daughter. What's more, he said, his niece had great respect for Gurudev, and she was willing to go to the *ashram*. The young woman stayed at the ashram for three weeks, and during that time the asthmatic condition vastly improved.

Various clergy members also came to the *ashram*, and they organized an All-Religions Group that met once a month, sometimes at the *ashram*, sometimes at a seminary, sometimes at the home of a Buddhist, and sometimes at an Islamic mosque.

By 1955, many devotees had come to regard Gurudev as their Guru, and they decided to form a new *ashram* in a nearby city called Kandy. They named the community, Satchidananda Thapovanam (*thapovanam* means forest of penance); and, while Mataji continued her service at the Divine Life Society's orphanage, this new *ashram* became the center for Gurudev's service. Students came from both the East and the West to learn the Yoga philosophy and practices. Those visitors left feeling revitalized and inspired; many letters like the one below described their experience:

It was with great pleasure that I spent three days with my children at Satchidananda Thapovanam, where they had lessons in Yoga *asanas* [postures]. The radiant personality of Swami Satchidanandaji brings renewed faith and hope to every heart. Spiritual equality for men and women of all religions is one of the greatest gifts of this peaceful *ashram*. My children and I offer our sincere and heartfelt thanks to all those who are here to help us in one way or other as a labor of love; indeed, for them it is a source of spiritual joy.

~ T. K. Wattegama

An atmosphere of spiritual unity prevailed at Satchidananda Thapovanam. A well-known Buddhist *bhikku* (monastic), Sri Ananda Maitreya, often brought his student *bhikkus* to visit Gurudev and to seek advice on the definitive text on Yoga, *The Yoga Sutras of Patanjali*. And monthly interfaith gatherings were held where Hindus, Buddhists, Catholics, and Muslims came together. One participant, Father Boudens, said of Gurudev, "He teaches people the way to happiness and peace of the heart."

Gurudev's everyday life embodied his teachings. For example, Father Boudens, who was a Belgian monk, described Gurudev's room and how it expressed his vision of the unity in diversity:

In Tennekumbura, a little outside of Kandy, lives one of the most well-known *sannyasis*, Swami Satchidananda, a beautiful apostle who could have come directly from the Passion Play of Oberammergau.

There he lives very simply, very humbly. No luxury. Nothing to get attached to. In a spacious room that occupies the largest part of his house, there are only the most necessary pieces of furniture: a small writing desk, a seat, and a small table with a couple of chairs to receive people who don't sit on the floor in the Eastern way. In the middle, everything is free. There on a mat, he does his Yoga postures and sits in meditation.

Against the wall one sees a few Hindu statues, a Buddha, and a crucifix. Also, a few sayings are hanging there; they give explanations about this strange mixture: "Truth is nobody's monopoly" and "Truth is one, but the ways that lead to it are many." The Swami is a Hindu, but he has a reverence for all other religions. He studies the holy scriptures of Buddhism. He reads the Bible. "One can learn from the founders of all religions," he says, "because they are all prophets. They speak in the name of God and manifest in their lives some of His qualities."

~ from *Sri Swami Satchidananda*

Eventually, centers sprang up all over Ceylon. So pleased was Swami Sivananda with the work of his disciple that he wrote to him from Rishikesh:

Through dynamic selfless service, you have won the hearts of the people of Ceylon. Your radiant personality and spiritual aura attract people to you; and your genuine humility and eagerness to serve all earns their admiration and affection. The newspaper reports reveal that your inspiring discourses command great respect and lead the men and women of Ceylon along the path of selflessness, unity, and dynamic service to the goal of peace and prosperity. I pray to the Lord to confer upon you continued radiant health and long life! May God bless you.

Chapter 5

A Soul on Wheels

He [Swami Satchidananda] was the pioneer of interfaith work.
He really lifted it up as the way to be—that there is one Creator,
one universe, one God. There are 900 million ways
of getting to that unity, and they all have to be respected.
And he was the one who really first gave language to that conviction.

~ The Very Reverend James Parks Morton,
Founder and Chair Emeritus of
the Interfaith Center of New York, and former Dean
of the Cathedral of St. John the Divine

While people came from near and far to visit the *ashram* and to study
Yoga with Gurudev, they also began to invite him to conduct classes
and to lecture at their own places. For example, Mr. Jean Belloir, the
French consul for Ceylon, invited Gurudev to offer classes at his
home. And Mr. Cecil Lyon, the American ambassador, and Mrs. Lyon
became interested in Yoga and asked Gurudev to teach monthly
classes in Hatha Yoga and meditation at their home for themselves,
for their friends, and for the people who served at the embassy.
Mr. Osmund De Silva, Inspector General of the Ceylon police and a
Buddhist, became a student and invited Gurudev to teach Hatha Yoga
classes to the men in the police training school. These marked only the
beginning of the thousands of invitations that Gurudev received and
accepted during the next fifty years.

In 1959, Gurudev was invited to lecture in Hong Kong. His tour
began with a three-day Yoga retreat that was held in an old Buddhist
monastery on Lantau, an island located twenty-five miles from Hong
Kong. The island had no road leading to the site, and there was
no electricity. But the retreat, attended by Buddhists, Hindus, and
Christians, was a great success, and Gurudev became known all over
Hong Kong.

Two years later, he undertook a more extensive Far Eastern tour; and this time he traveled not only to Hong Kong, but also to Japan, the Philippines, and Malaysia. In Manila, Gurudev met again with Mr. Jean Belloir, who had left Ceylon to become the French consul for the Philippines. Mr. Belloir arranged for Gurudev to address the Breakfast Club, a distinguished group whose president was the president of the Philippines. Among the many members who turned out for the talk, two Catholic priests stayed afterward to speak with Gurudev. The two men approached Gurudev, and one said, "Swami, do you know that you have really converted us?" Gurudev smiled, thanking the priest for his sentiments, but he explained that he couldn't accept those sentiments, because, he said, he hadn't come to convert anyone. Gurudev told the father that maybe what had occurred was not conversion but absorption; that is, the priest had more likely absorbed the teachings that Gurudev had shared. Warmly embracing Gurudev, the priests acknowledged that Gurudev was correct—and that he really did have a way with words.

What became obvious to the priests was not only Gurudev's natural ability to teach the Yoga philosophy and practices from which he had benefited and in which he himself was absorbed. They also realized that, while he willingly shared his knowledge, experience, and insights with those who sought them, he was not proselytizing. In fact, Gurudev never invited himself to lecture anywhere or to anyone. He went only when and where he was invited. And he knew that the philosophy of Yoga, as well as the practices, did not undermine but only enhanced one's own spiritual beliefs. The priests, apparently, also understood that.

Another anecdote from the 1960s reflects Gurudev's universal point of view, as well as his candidness. At the time, Yvonne Hanneman was a young American filmmaker who traveled to the East on a Fulbright scholarship in order to research and document folk art. In Ceylon she visited the bazaars in search of authentic folk art, but all she could find were cheap souvenirs made of plastic and rubber. She discovered, though, that beautiful handmade objects were to be found at religious festivals. In fact, the pieces of folk art that people made and brought as offerings to God were, as Hanneman described them, "fresh and alive." Thus, religious festivals became the source for her research and because she had always been interested in a philosophical view of life, it was easy for her to adapt. She had already read about reincarnation, and she became immersed in the pervading spiritual atmosphere of the East.

Hanneman had been referred to several Hindu swamis from whom she might gather information, but, somehow, none of them quite appealed to her. A friend then suggested that she meet Swami Satchidananda. Swami Satchidananda, Yvonne's friend told her, could tell her all that she needed to know, and she'd be happy to take her to his *ashram*.

Although Hanneman felt nervous when she first met Gurudev, as he answered her questions, clearly and simply, she began to feel comfortable. In fact, she found the experience so rewarding that when she ran out of questions, she began inventing more. She was impressed.

At one point, Hanneman gave Gurudev a couple of rolls of color film as a token of her appreciation for his answering all her questions. She chose the film because they had discussed photography, and she knew that film was a rare commodity in Ceylon at that time.

One day, she went to a Buddhist festival, the Perahera Festival in Kandy. The main attractions at that grand festival were the colorful Buddhist and Kandyan dances and the procession of lavishly decorated elephants. Walking backward down the street, photographing the approaching elephants, she kept taking steps until suddenly she bumped into someone. She turned around, and there was Gurudev, completely laden down with cameras, light meters, and movie film. With a big smile, he shouted, "I'm using your film!" Hanneman thought to herself, "How wonderful. This is a real swami who can make the jump between East and West, not held down by all the Eastern customs and patterns. He's so practical."

Yvonne Hanneman's insight foreshadowed Gurudev's future in the West. And she wasn't the only one to sense that Gurudev's service would be far-ranging and unencumbered by cultural conventions.

One morning at the Kandy *ashram*, Mrs. Rasiah went to see Gurudev; she found him in a pensive mood. "I am seeing a vision," he told her. "I am seated in a large glass globe, and globes with glowing shrines of all religions are rotating around that central globe." He revealed to her his wish that the whole world might come together, that people would love one another in spite of superficial differences, and that they would pray to the universal light, each one according to his or her own beliefs.

According to Mrs. Rasiah, Gurudev was her "Star of Bethlehem," because his light showed the location of the truth. And that's why she replied, "The risen star has come more than halfway around the world and has only a little more distance to cover."

This conversation took place in 1966; but we've jumped ahead of ourselves.

CHAPTER 6

To Everything There Is a Season

My heart's mirror was polished by love,
and then I began to understand the mysteries.
I rose out of my inner darkness and became
the Light for all to see.
Some say the path is difficult,
but for me it went so easily.

~ Sharab Nawaz, Sufi poet

When Gurudev lived in Ceylon, the island country was a veritable paradise. With its lovely climate and gorgeous landscape it drew many tourists, and many of the Western visitors made their way to Satchidananda Thapovanam to see Gurudev. Invariably, after spending time with him, these Westerners would urge Gurudev to come to the West. And he would always reply, "Fine, fine. If God wants that, certainly I will do it." Then the tourists would return to their countries with all their souvenirs and photographs, and the matter would end there. But life means change, and change was in the air.

The Bible tells us, "There is a time for everything and a season for every activity under the heavens (Ecclesiastes 3:1)." And as Gurudev put it: "There is a divine plan behind everything. If we allow ourselves to be used as good instruments by that Unseen Force, many things can happen in a mysterious, miraculous way. If we interfere by introducing our own plan, the egocentric plan, tension will be created. In any event, ultimately, the Divine Plan will win out." One evening in 1965, at Satchidananda Thapovanam, a divine plan began to unfold.

On that evening, Gurudev was holding *satsang* when the ring of the telephone interrupted him. Fred De Silva, Kandy's deputy mayor and a devotee of Gurudev's, was calling. Deputy Mayor De Silva told Gurudev that he was hosting an American named Conrad Rooks, who had an interest in Yoga and wished to meet with him. Mr. De Silva was wondering when Gurudev might be able to see this young man. Gurudev replied that the young man could come right away to the *satsang*, but the deputy mayor said that the American did not want to meet him in front of others; he wanted to see him quietly, all by himself. Could the young American come later that evening? Gurudev gave his consent.

Conrad Rooks arrived at 10 p.m. He sat down on the floor, assuming a cross-legged position, and he said that he just wanted to ask one or two questions about *pranayama* (yogic breathing practices), *kundalini* (the creative force said to be located in the subtle body, around the base of the spine), and *japa* (the repetition of a mantra)—subjects not usually taken up by novices. Gurudev remarked that Conrad seemed to know quite a bit already and asked him what his doubts were. He proceeded to answer Conrad's questions, one by one, finally explaining that those practices did not constitute the entirety of Yoga but were only aids. Yoga, he told his guest, is meant to be practiced throughout one's life, twenty-four hours a day. That is, a person can't be a yogi for half an hour and a non-yogi at all other times. At that point, Conrad relaxed, the tension that he had held in his face drained away, and he and Gurudev continued their discussion until after midnight.

After two weeks of learning the techniques of *pranayama* and *japa*, the new devotee decided to stay with Gurudev for at least three months, and he continued to visit the *ashram* daily for instruction and discussion. After ten days, though, he received a cable from his Paris office. He was a professional filmmaker, and he was being asked to return in order to take care of some urgent business matters. Rooks left for Paris. More than a month later, Gurudev received a call from someone in the British Airways office in Colombo telling him that a round-trip ticket to Paris was waiting for him there; that he just needed to choose a date of departure. The ticket had been purchased by Conrad Rooks, who sent Gurudev a cable inviting him to come to Paris and to take a two-month holiday in Europe.

He agreed to go to Europe for a month.

It was Eastertime, and on the way to Paris Gurudev stopped in Cairo, Jerusalem, and Rome. Father Joachim Pillai of the Kandy seminary, a good friend of Gurudev's, wrote a letter of introduction to Father Benoit, a Dominican monk in Jerusalem who headed the research group of a Bible school. Father Benoit replied that he would arrange for Gurudev's accommodations in the holy city. When Gurudev arrived at the mission, Father Benoit went across the street to the hotel to check on the room that he'd reserved for the visitor. While Gurudev waited, the mission's abbot came in and introduced himself. When the father returned, the abbot told him that Gurudev need not stay in a hotel; he could stay in the mission for as long as he liked.

Gurudev was led to a room that opened onto a view of the entire city, with its churches, synagogues, mosques, and bazaars. During his stay, he attended mass and held discussions with and gave lectures to the mission fathers.

> My encounter with Swami Satchidananda was very short but impressive. We had some good conversations about Yoga and spiritual life. I asked him for advice about Hatha Yoga *asanas* that I had tried to practice myself, and he asked me to take him to the Holy Sepulchre of Christ.
>
> I asked him if he would like to see other places.... "No," he replied, "only the Church of the Cross and the Resurrection." We went there, and I was very impressed by the way he knelt before the place of the cross and prayed with deep concentration. When we went out into the streets, people were astonished by the sight of his colorful dress. Some said, "He's a rabbi!" Others said, "Oh! Look at Jesus Christ." He smiled and told me, "Do not pay attention. I am used to that."
>
> These days were short, but we grew to be good friends.
>
> ~ Pierre Benoit, O. P.

Yogendra Duraiswamy, who, at the time, was the Ceylonese ambassador to Rome, knew Gurudev well. One day, as they sat talking in Mr. Duraiswamy's drawing room, the ambassador asked Gurudev whether he'd like to meet the pope, Paul VI. Gurudev appreciated the idea. Normally, private audiences with the Holy Father took a week to arrange, but since Gurudev was leaving Rome the next day, the cardinal in charge, Cardinal Morello, asked to meet with Gurudev first for a chat; then, he would decide about an audience with the pope. Cardinal Morello wanted to meet with Gurudev immediately.

Gurudev and Mr. Duraiswamy arrived at the cardinal's Vatican office as soon as possible that day, and what was to have been a twenty-minute meeting stretched into two hours. Gurudev answered the cardinal's questions about Yoga and about the Hindu religion; and when the visit ended, Cardinal Morello said, "I haven't met a person like you before. I think that you and the Holy Father must meet one another. I'll arrange for your private audience tomorrow."

The following day, Gurudev and the ambassador returned to the Vatican. Gurudev had thought about the proper way to greet a pope, and he decided to greet him in the traditional Indian fashion. They walked through the long, high halls until they reached the Holy Father. Gurudev took out a lime and offered it to him. The pontiff was rather surprised. He asked, "What does this lime signify?" Gurudev replied, "When Hindus go to meet a sage, a swami, or a saintly person, they bring a lime. It symbolizes an offering and, at the same time, it has a beneficial medicinal effect on the system. When you sit for a long time in meditation, a great deal of heat is produced. Bile secretion develops. The lime juice cools the system and serves as a remedy."

With a smile, the pope accepted the gift.

Gurudev praised the Holy Father's efforts to promote understanding among all Christians. Then he suggested, "Now, why don't you come forward to bring the entire world together—all people, regardless of religious or racial differences? It is not only the Christians who should come together. All people should unite in the name of religious harmony. Your word could carry a great deal of weight in helping people realize the oneness of the spirit."

What an auspicious beginning to Gurudev's interfaith service in the West! Evidently, the divine plan was proceeding according to schedule.

At last Gurudev flew to Paris to meet with Conrad Rooks. One afternoon, nine weeks after he'd left Kandy, he and Conrad were chatting about different religions. The filmmaker told Gurudev about his trip to Mount Athos, a peninsula in Greece cut off from the conveniences of the modern world. Surrounded by the Aegean Sea and home to a great number of monasteries, its only inhabitants were monks. No women, not even female animals, were allowed to set foot on its soil. Conrad tried to describe its unique environment, but he eventually concluded that his words could not do justice to the beauty and peacefulness of Mount Athos, so he decided to take Gurudev there to experience it first-hand.

To make the journey, it was necessary to obtain a special letter from Greece's cultural ministry and a permit from the monks of Mount Athos. Conrad's secretary made arrangements for transportation and accommodations. Gurudev stayed at the oldest and largest of the twenty monasteries on the peninsula, where he discovered that many similarities existed between Hindu monastic customs and the way in which these monks lived: they arose early in the morning for meditation, they never ate meat, and they were celibate. When he asked the priests to explain the reason for the regulation concerning women and female animals, though, none of them seemed to know. They simply said that it was a custom, and they didn't seem very interested in the matter. Although Gurudev had the utmost respect for these monks and their path, he questioned the wisdom of a custom that called for the monks' complete avoidance of even the most reserved contact with their sisters in God's family.

Throughout his life, Gurudev showed genuine reverence for the beliefs and customs of all traditions, but he never hesitated to question and to explore the reasoning or the motivation behind them.

CHAPTER 7

The Light of One Candle

*Thousands of candles can be lighted from a single candle,
and the life of the candle will not be shortened.
Happiness never decreases by being shared.*

~ Buddha

After spending fourteen weeks in Europe, meeting with Yoga students, lecturing, and teaching, Gurudev informed Conrad that it was time for him to return to the *ashram* in Kandy. Conrad's response: "Swamiji, I've been watching you. I've seen so many Westerners benefit from your presence. Instead of going straight back to Ceylon, why don't you go around the other way and visit my country also? Then, you can fly back via Japan." Although Gurudev wasn't really prepared to make such a journey, he felt that if Conrad thought it worthwhile, he'd do it. Gurudev had observed for many years how the Divine worked through him, how he was simply an instrument. So, at least for the time being, he calmly placed his destiny in Conrad's hands, and Conrad's secretary exchanged Gurudev's ticket home for one that would take him around the world.

Swami Sivananda taught that one of the most invaluable spiritual practices was to "adapt, adjust, and accommodate." Gurudev was soon graced with the opportunity to do just that, to "go with the flow," as the hippies of the era would put it. Conrad had reconsidered his idea that Gurudev travel to the United States. America, he told Gurudev, is a "crazy, crazy country." Conrad felt that if Gurudev spent any time in the country, he'd probably develop a poor opinion of Americans. He didn't want that, so he recommended that Gurudev return to Ceylon.

They had to wait three days for the new reservation to be confirmed, and during that time a young New York artist named Peter Max arrived in Paris to do some publicity work for Conrad's film *Chappaqua*. Peter stayed in Paris for two weeks, working and visiting with Gurudev, asking him lots of questions about Yoga. At one point, he realized that his work on the film was not as important as his meetings with Gurudev. He questioned Gurudev about Yoga, and, as he remembers it, he thought about the answers all day long. One day, he announced to Gurudev: "America needs you."

Peter Max felt strongly that Gurudev should come to New York City so that more Americans could meet him. In truth, Gurudev had no desire to go anywhere, but he told Peter, "If Providence wants me to go, I'll go." Peter's response: "I think I'll pray for your visit."

Meanwhile, Conrad had reconsidered, and, once again, he felt that Gurudev should indeed visit the United States, although, this time, he suggested that Gurudev avoid New York and fly straight to California. His assessment: Gurudev would find America an agreeable place as long as he did not visit New York.

On his way to the U.S., Gurudev made a stopover in London to meet his old friend, the Buddhist *bhikku* from Ceylon, who had come to Gurudev in order to learn about *The Yoga Sutras of Patanjali*, a collection of aphorisms that embody the ancient Yoga teachings and practices.

Together they visited the Buddhist center in London. It happened that the monk who headed the Buddhist center in West Berlin was visiting there at the same time. Impressed by Gurudev, the monk invited him to return with him to Germany to give some talks at his center.

While Gurudev was gone, Conrad had once more reconsidered his travel recommendations. Realizing that people would not think well of him if they learned that he had dissuaded Gurudev from visiting New York, he suggested that Gurudev go to New York after all, at least for the sake of seeing it.

Gurudev arrived in New York on July 31, 1966; and, not surprising, the originally planned two-day stopover came and went. At first, Gurudev stayed with Peter and Liz Max and their young child in the Max family's small apartment, where every evening a number of visitors came to observe and to listen to him. Within a short time, so many people began to crowd into the apartment that the group forming around Gurudev recognized that he would have to relocate. One of the members invited Gurudev to stay at his more spacious flat.

While he was glad to see the keen interest in Yoga, Gurudev also came to understand Conrad's warnings about New York. The visitors who came to see him smoked cigarettes, blowing smoke in his face; often, they were "tripping" on LSD or "stoned" on marijuana or hashish.

Nonetheless, Gurudev patiently accepted their behavior. His rationale: "Though these American children didn't seem to know how to behave, I could see that they were seeking. I wouldn't expect such treatment in India, but this wasn't India. Sometimes, I would think, 'Is this the way they behave in front of their own clergy?' Then, I would accept it, knowing that they were sincere seekers."

It was the sixties, after all, the era of the counterculture and a period of great turmoil in America. Young people were rebelling against "the Establishment," whose values they found to be hypocritical and meaningless. Some tried to escape the system by using drugs; others used violence to fight against the system; and some chose peaceful, nonviolent means like marches and protests. In that atmosphere of confusion and unrest, many so-called flower children found their way to the peaceful swami from India who was sharing the teachings of Yoga in a modest apartment on the Upper West Side of Manhattan.

Eventually, the crowds of visitors who came to see Gurudev grew too big for even that apartment.

The students wanted Gurudev to stay longer, so they resolved to find him a bigger space. Gurudev wondered whether their interest would actually be sustained if he were not around, and he decided to test them. He agreed to extend his stay for a few more weeks. But he also announced that while they looked for another apartment, he would travel to Montreal to visit Swami Vishnudevananda, his brother monk, and that when the apartment was ready, they should phone him. Since Gurudev's original ticket was marked only "Montreal, Canada," the new disciples exchanged the ticket for one with a return flight to New York. They wanted to make sure that Gurudev would come back to them. And within four days, the New York disciples called Gurudev to let him know that a new apartment was ready for him.

Located in the Oliver Cromwell Hotel on West 72nd Street, the apartment had a spacious living room capable of accommodating large discussion groups and Hatha Yoga classes, a kitchen, and a bathroom. They'd reserved the place, they told Gurudev, for *only* three months, and when Gurudev countered, "*Only* three months?" they assured him that if he couldn't stay that long, then they'd cancel the reservation.

It wasn't long, however, before even this apartment was too small. Undaunted, the group set out yet again to search for a larger place. They found an old, nine-room apartment at 500 West End Avenue, called a meeting immediately, and scraped together enough money for the rent and security deposit. When Gurudev learned of this new venture and asked for how long they had rented the apartment, he learned that they had signed a three-year lease. He reminded them that he would very soon be returning to Ceylon, but they were undeterred: "We're not going to detain you. Please feel free to go whenever you wish."

The scene was set for the establishment of the first Integral Yoga® Institute. Hatha Yoga classes were scheduled on a regular and permanent basis. Friday evenings were set aside for lectures. Gurudev trained one of the disciples, a schoolteacher named Lakshmi, to teach Hatha Yoga, and he alternated teaching with her. She also acted as secretary and treasurer for the organization that was rapidly forming around Gurudev. Each month, eleven of the original members pooled their money to pay the rent. Members began working on incorporating the organization, which now needed to be named. Gurudev assured them that any name they chose would be fine. They presented him with a list of proposed names, including Satchidananda Sangha and Satchidananda Center; he suggested calling the organization the Divine Life Society. But one of the devotees insisted that Americans had grown tired of such terms as *divine*. They did agree, though, to his proposal that they include the word *Yoga* somewhere in the name.

When they came up with "Satchidananda Yoga Sangha" (the Sanskrit word *sangha* means community, assembly, and company), Gurudev remarked that their teaching was an integral one, a synthesis. He also mentioned that his spiritual master, Swami Sivananda, used the term *integral* very often to describe the teachings that they were presenting and suggested that the phrase "Integral Yoga" be included in the name of their organization.

After much deliberation, the group decided on Integral Yoga Center, but Gurudev piped up again: Why don't we call it Integral Yoga Institute? IYI. Two years later, Yvonne Hanneman, the photographer who had visited him in Ceylon, was leafing through some notes in Gurudev's Ceylon diary. On one page there appeared a proposal for a new *ashram* and center. Printed in large letters were the words *Integral Yoga Institute*.

The IYI grew through word of mouth. Someone would attend one of Gurudev's lectures, and the following week he or she would bring several friends. Many began to practice Hatha Yoga and meditation. Some aspired to a deeper connection with Gurudev, whom they began to think of as their *guru*, or spiritual guide. And to those who sincerely wanted this connection, Gurudev gave mantra initiation, whereby the disciple takes the preceptor as his or her spiritual guide and is given a mantra, or sacred sound on which to meditate.

Finally, though, as Christmas drew closer, Gurudev called the IYI members together to announce that it was time for him to return to Ceylon and the devotees there who had been waiting months for his return. The New Yorkers were eager to know when Gurudev would come back to the United States, but he advised them not to assume that he'd be coming back; he had to think of the disciples in Ceylon, too. He reminded them that America was a country where life changed quickly and that, in a few months, they might forget about him. It's possible, he said, that Yoga might be only a passing fancy and that, before long, they might grow tired of it. The new devotees nonetheless promised to continue with their service and their practices, giving classes and listening to tapes of Gurudev's lectures while he was gone. They appealed to him to finish his work in Ceylon and then return to New York permanently. Gurudev couldn't promise that, because to him it all depended on where the need was the greatest. But he did say, "We'll see what happens."

In January, Gurudev left New York for Chicago, where he stayed at the Ramakrishna-Vivekananda Center. Near the center, there was a convent, and when the sisters learned of Gurudev's arrival, they invited him to come to their cloister to speak about Yoga. As Gurudev described it, entering the convent was like entering a high-security prison. The visitor walked through one door to a hall; a peephole quickly opened and shut; he walked through a second door that closed tightly behind him and then went through a third door.

Finally, he entered a small room. He was asked to sit on a chair directly in front of a window. On the other side of the window were a number of seats; Gurudev likened his situation to television watching. He watched as the black-clad sisters filed into the room on the other side of the window. The sister in charge sat directly in front of him. Gurudev began to speak about Yoga, its aims and its benefits, and at the end of his talk he asked, "Sister, why must these nuns always be confined?" The sister in charge hesitated for a moment, anxiously glancing at the nuns seated behind her. Then she explained, "They're being trained. They spend most of their time in meditation."

> "Yes, I know," replied Gurudev. "But why can't they come out and see how the world is? They seem to be kept completely away from the world as if it were a dangerous place for them. That will create the wrong impression about the world outside. Moving about in the world and performing service should strengthen the conviction of a monk or a nun, while hiding from the world will often make for a weak foundation."

The sister in charge looked at the other nuns and then back to Gurudev. But he continued.

"I don't think that it's a natural growth. It's something like keeping a plant indoors without fresh air or sunlight. That plant will not have a natural growth. It will become pale and lose its color. The world itself is a big university. There is a lot to learn from it. They should be allowed out now and then to see what's happening there and to test their reactions. Then, they can return to seclusion and analyze their feelings."

While the faces behind the glass lit up, the sister in charge seemed a bit shaken, and she leaned toward the glass, lowering her voice:

"Swamiji! You should not tell them all these things. We can talk about it privately. They've already brought such ideas forward, and now you're just stirring them up."

Undaunted and maintaining his previous voice level, Gurudev went on:

"That's fine; that's good. They should do that. They should bring up such things."

"But, Swamiji," the nun persisted, "we have to listen to the hierarchy. We can't just do what we want."

"Well," countered Gurudev, "make the hierarchy aware of the situation here. Unless they know there is a problem, they won't do anything about it. 'Ask; it shall be given.' The child must cry so that the mother will know that it's hungry and can feed it."

From his many years of experience as a renunciate, reclusive and otherwise, Gurudev knew that for some monastics, no matter their religious tradition, a completely solitary life led in silence was natural. He also recognized that for most seekers, retreating from the world was not meant to be an end in itself; rather, it was a practice intended to prepare the spiritual aspirant to be "in the world but not of it;" that is, to serve one and all joyfully, peacefully, and selflessly without being attached to the fruits of one's actions.

Certainly, Gurudev respected the spiritual traditions of the sisters' Catholic faith, but he also recognized that strict adherence to dogma without consideration of the physical and emotional needs of the nuns would produce tension rather than the peaceful atmosphere they sought to create. His empathy, his compassion, his understanding of human nature, and his commitment to serving others prompted him to speak frankly and freed him of the fear that many of us might have had of appearing to be politically incorrect.

This was not the last invitation that Gurudev would receive from Catholic nuns. A couple of years later, in 1969, the nuns of the St. Augustine convent in Quebec City, Canada, invited Gurudev to conduct a three-day seminar, during which he gave lectures, led Hatha Yoga classes, held discussions, and even gave mantra initiation to thirty-five nuns who requested it.

In February 1967, almost a year since he had left for his "one-month trip" to the West, Gurudev returned to Ceylon. Hundreds of friends and devotees greeted him at the airport in Colombo, and they held receptions for him in Kandy, Trincomalee, and Jaffna. When he arrived at his cottage, he found a pile of letters waiting for him. They all conveyed, more or less, the same sentiments as expressed in the following examples:

> The members of the IYI have asked me to write and urge you to come back as soon as possible.

And,

> There has been a mass spiritual awakening and a coming together of all people who can sense this. Thousands of people gathered in Central Park for a "be-in" just to be together. There was meditation, chanting, dancing, kite flying, loving, and everybody dressed in colorful clothes with flowers and feathers. The only thing missing was our Swamiji. Come back soon! We all love you very much.

Furthermore, when Gurudev met with Cecil Lyon, the American ambassador, and his wife, even the ambassador requested that he return to the United States. He had been to the States and had visited the Integral Yoga Institute, and he had seen the work that was being done. He, too, felt that Gurudev's presence was really needed there.

In order to make the right decision, Gurudev meditated on the situation. It seemed to him that God was guiding him to return to America. Apparently, the people there were sincerely yearning for spiritual guidance. They were asking for help in the manner that Gurudev had described to the nuns in Chicago: "When the child cries, the mother will recognize the hunger and feed it." He realized, also, that the sincere devotees in Ceylon already knew the yogic teachings quite well and that there were other *sannyasis* there to guide them if the need arose. His decision was made. He would stay in Ceylon until mid-April in order to celebrate the Tamil and Singhalese New Year with the devotees.

In the meantime, Gurudev accepted an invitation from Conrad Rooks to join him in visiting Lama Govinda in Almora, a hill station dotted with temples. The lama made a profound impression on Gurudev, who described him in this way: "In Lama Govinda I saw a great scholar and authority on Tibetan Buddhism. Because of his constant involvement in Tibetan scriptures and practices, he has imbibed all that great peace and serenity."

After visiting with Lama Govinda, Gurudev and Conrad traveled on to Benares, Katmandu, and then down to Dharamsala for a meeting with the Dalai Lama.

His Holiness, the fourteenth Dalai Lama, a slight, delicate, young man with glowing eyes, sat on a chair. Conrad Rooks recalled that he felt like "a tiny intruder at a meeting between two giants." Gurudev asked the Dalai Lama about the psychedelic interpretations of the various Tibetan Yoga books, because this way of looking at the ancient teachings was quite popular in the West at the time. The revered holy man replied, "No drug can give you these experiences. They can be reached only by going deep into meditation and not by any external agency."

"What about the opening of the third eye?" continued Gurudev. "There are books that claim this can be achieved by an operation."

The Dalai Lama answered unequivocally, "There is no external action involved. The third eye exists not on the physical plane but on the more subtle, spiritual level. It can be experienced only through deep meditation." Clearly, he didn't approve of the modern interpretations of the ancient, secret Tibetan practices. And perhaps Gurudev posed these questions for Conrad's benefit, to educate him, since Gurudev himself had known the answers all along.

Later on, Gurudev remarked, "I could feel sanctity in the Dalai Lama. Although he appeared a bit young and modern, one could feel a higher spiritual experience pervading him. I felt a great deal of warmth in his presence."

CHAPTER 8

The New World

But it does me no injury for my neighbor
to say there are twenty gods or no God.
It neither picks my pocket nor breaks my leg.

~ Thomas Jefferson,
Query XVII of Notes on the State of Virginia

Gurudev returned to New York on May 24, 1967. In September of that year, the IYI members and other students celebrated the birthday of Swami Sivananda at New York's Village Theater. Two thousand people came to the tribute to watch dance performances, listen to musical offerings from both the Indian and Western traditions, and hear Gurudev speak. His wisdom, unconditional love, and universal outlook had evidently penetrated the hearts of seekers from diverse backgrounds and traditions. Gurudev's interfaith approach to peace was taking hold in the New World.

Centuries ago, when it came to interfaith interaction, bright spots were few, because open-mindedness was subordinate to competition in trade and the acquisition of resources. According to "A Brief History of the Interfaith Movement," an essay published by the Interfaith Settlement Foundation, during ancient times much of the religious interaction was based on the rise and fall of empires and nations (including the Greek, Chinese, Persian, Roman, Gothic, Nordic, Mongolian, Khmer, Songhai, Moorish, Zulu, Arowak, Aztec, Maya, Inca, Iroquois, Lakotah, Ottoman, English, French, Spanish, Japanese, German, Russian, and others) and the expanding diasporas (for example, the Judaic, Hindu, Buddhist, Christian, Muslim, and Sikh) that emerged through these temporal fluctuations.

That essay also describes how, during the 19th century, this historical pattern begins to alter as interaction between countries increases, especially between Eastern and Western nations. Thus, such figures as Sri Ramakrishna and his disciple, Swami Vivekananda, emerge in India. And in Persia, we find Bahá'u'lláh and the new international, interreligious Bahá'í faith. In the West, groups like the Unitarians and the Universalists appear. Later on, the work of such scholars as Max Müller and Rhys Davids fosters interfaith understanding through their translations of Hindu and Buddhist scriptures, respectively.

The real beginning of the interfaith movement as we know it today occurred when representatives of the various world religions came together in 1893 at the first Parliament of the World's Religions, held at the World's Columbian Exposition in Chicago. A momentous event, the parliament provided religious leaders and devotees from the different religions, including Hinduism, Judaism, Buddhism, Christianity, Islam, Jainism, and Bahá'í, with an opportunity to engage in dialogue and to learn from one another. It was at this groundbreaking event that Swami Vivekananda gave the following brief speech, one so compelling that it brought the audience to its feet for an ovation:

Sisters and Brothers of America,

It fills my heart with joy unspeakable to rise in response to the warm and cordial welcome which you have given us. I thank you in the name of the most ancient order of monks in the world; I thank you in the name of the mother of religions; and I thank you in the name of the millions and millions of Hindu people of all classes and sects. My thanks, also, to some of the speakers on this platform who, referring to the delegates from the Orient, have told you that these men from far-off nations may well claim the honor of bearing to different lands the idea of toleration.

I am proud to belong to a religion which has taught the world both tolerance and universal acceptance. We believe not only in universal toleration, but we accept all religions as true.

I am proud to belong to a nation which has sheltered the persecuted and the refugees of all religions and all nations of the earth. I am proud to tell you that we have gathered in our bosom the purest remnant of the Israelites, who came to southern India and took refuge with us in the very year in which their holy temple was shattered to pieces by Roman tyranny.

I am proud to belong to the religion which has sheltered and is still fostering the remnant of the grand Zoroastrian nation. I will quote to you, brethren, a few lines from a hymn which I remember to have repeated from my earliest boyhood, which is every day repeated by millions of human beings:

As the different streams having their sources in different places
all mingle their water in the sea, so, O Lord, the different paths
which men take through different tendencies, various though they
appear, crooked or straight, all lead to Thee.

The present convention, which is one of the most august assemblies ever held, is in itself a vindication, a declaration to the world, of the wonderful doctrine preached in the *Gita*:

Whosoever comes to Me, through whatsoever form, I reach him;
all men are struggling through paths which in the end lead to Me.

Sectarianism, bigotry, and its horrible descendant, fanaticism, have long possessed this beautiful earth. They have filled the earth with violence, drenched it often and often with human blood, destroyed civilization, and sent whole nations to despair. Had it not been for these horrible demons, human society would be far more advanced than it is now. But their time is come; and I fervently hope that the bell that tolled this morning in honor of this convention may be the death-knell of all fanaticism, of all persecutions with the sword or with the pen, and of all uncharitable feelings between persons wending their way to the same goal.

This auspicious occasion led to the creation, in 1900, of the International Association for Religious Freedom, in Boston, Massachusetts, which continues to function to this day as the oldest interfaith organization in the world.

According to the Reverend Dr. Marcus Braybrooke—a retired Anglican parish priest, president of the World Congress of Faiths, an interfaith colleague, friend, and signer with Gurudev and many other interfaith clergy of the Global Ethic Foundation's "Declaration toward a Global Ethic"—it was Charles Caroll Bonney, a distinguished lawyer and a follower of the Swedish theologian Emanuel Swedenborg (1688–1772), who, in 1889, came up with the idea of the Parliament of the World's Religions. In an illuminating article, "A Dream That Is Contagious" (*Interfaith Observer*, www.interfaithobserver.org, October 10, 2011), Reverend Braybrooke discusses the first, 19th-century parliament and then traces the creation and evolution of interfaith organizations for the next hundred years, up to the present day. He reports that nowadays the greatest growth of the interfaith movement is happening at the grassroots level. Activities are being organized locally by people who want to get to know their neighbors better.

The burgeoning interfaith movement took root in the United States, a multicultural nation that itself embodies the concept of unity in diversity. Interreligious dialogue and interaction between liberal-minded religious leaders and followers of different faiths continued, research was carried out, and papers written. "A Brief History of the Interfaith Movement"—an essay appearing on the website www.interfaithsettlement.org—points out, with the creation of international institutions like the United Nations, founded in 1945 and housed in New York City, the interfaith movement became increasingly dynamic.

And in 1960, Judith (Juliet) Hollister, who would later become a close friend and associate of Gurudev's, founded the Temple of Understanding. Based in New York and created as a medium for interfaith dialogue and understanding, the organization gained the support of such prominent figures as Eleanor Roosevelt, Prime Minister Jawaharlal Nehru of India, Pope John XXIII, President Anwar el Sadat of Egypt, the fourteenth Dalai Lama, Albert Schweitzer, and Swami Satchidananda, who became one of its advisors. It was not surprising that the United States proved to be fertile ground for the propagation of the interfaith movement, for the seed of that movement was planted by Thomas Jefferson and his fellow founding fathers when they campaigned for religious freedom more than two centuries earlier.

Following the lead of his illustrious predecessors, President Barack Obama, in 2010, reinforced America's commitment to religious freedom as he stepped into the controversy surrounding plans for an Islamic center to be built on a site near New York City's Ground Zero memorial to those who died during the September 11, 2001, destruction of the World Trade Center: "This is America. And our commitment to religious freedom must be unshakable. The principle that people of all faiths are welcome in this country and that they will not be treated differently by their government is essential to who we are." As the historian Kenneth C. Davis points out in "America's True History of Religious Tolerance," an essay that appeared in the October 2010 issue of *Smithsonian* magazine, in making these comments President Obama was paying "homage to a vision that politicians and preachers have extolled for more than two centuries—that America historically has been a place of religious tolerance." Davis reminds us that, just a few blocks from Ground Zero, George Washington himself had voiced the same sentiment. Davis questions whether this sentiment is grounded in reality, remarking that most Americans learn the "fairy tale" version of history in school.

As the familiar story goes, the Pilgrims who sailed from England on the *Mayflower* in 1620 came to America in search of religious freedom. And, the tale continues, ever since the Pilgrims arrived, millions of people from around the world have come to the melting pot that is America in order to be free to practice their own faiths. Davis argues, however, that the problem with this "tidy narrative" is that it's a myth—the American myth. He contends that the real story of religion in America is "an often awkward, frequently embarrassing and occasionally bloody tale that most civics books and high school texts either paper over or shunt to the side." And there are many examples: discrimination, suppression, and even the murder of "heretics" and "unbelievers," foreigners and natives, for instance.

The Pilgrims and Puritans in New England in the early 1600s had fled religious persecution in England, but they themselves were intolerant of religious views opposed to their own. In fact, they wanted to set up a theocracy. Thus, the famous Puritan dissidents Anne Hutchinson and Roger Williams were banished because of their disagreements over theology and politics. Catholics were banished from Puritan Boston, and, along with other non-Puritans, they were also banned from the colonies. Four Quakers were hanged in Boston between 1659 and 1661 simply because they continued to return to the city to stand up for their rights. Davis also maintains that anti-Catholic feelings contributed to the revolutionary mood in America after King George III "extended an olive branch to French Catholics in Canada with the Quebec Act of 1774, which recognized their religion."

After the Revolution, only Christians were allowed to hold public office, and Catholics could do so only after renouncing the papal authority. In 1777, New York banned Catholics from public office (a policy that continued until 1806). In Maryland, Catholics had full civil rights, but Jews did not.

In the midst of such virulent discrimination, Thomas Jefferson, governor of Virginia at the time, drafted a bill in 1779 that guaranteed equality for citizens of all religions who lived in that state, including those who practiced no religion. It was around that time that Jefferson wrote the quote that opens this chapter: "[I]t does me no injury for my neighbor to say there are twenty gods or no God. It neither picks my pocket nor breaks my leg." But Jefferson's plan did not move forward until several years later.

In his essay, Davis tells how James Madison, who later became known as the father of the Constitution, also took up the cause for religious freedom, laying out in a carefully crafted essay entitled "Memorial and Remonstrance Against Religious Assessments" the reasons why supporting Christian instruction was not the business of the state. Madison's petition was signed by some 2,000 Virginians, and his argument became a fundamental component of American philosophy. Among the fifteen points set out in it was his declaration that "the Religion . . . of every man must be left to the conviction and conscience of every . . . man to exercise it as these may dictate. This right is in its nature an inalienable right."

Eventually, in 1786, the Virginia Act for Establishing Religious Freedom, a somewhat modified version of Jefferson's original draft of the bill, became law. After it was passed, Jefferson wrote that the law "meant to comprehend, within the mantle of its protection, the Jew, the Gentile, the Christian and the Mahometan, the Indoo and Infidel of every denomination." (It is worth noting that the term *infidel*, used here in its neutral meaning of one who does not believe in religion or one who believes in a religion other than one's own, has been and still is deployed in a negative sense by fundamentalists whose reactionary thinking reflects bigotry born of ignorance and, concomitantly, fear of the unknown.)

To move ahead, to evolve, whether as individuals or as nations, we must confront past attitudes and actions and consider their consequences. Self-inquiry enables us to develop the power of discrimination necessary for us to make wise decisions. It is always challenging—for an individual as well as a nation—to analyze the past objectively, to evaluate attitudes and actions with detachment. And it is equally challenging to integrate into the reality of our daily lives the values idealized in our myths.

It was the recognition and examination of past divisiveness that allowed Presidents Washington, Jefferson, Adams, and Madison to push ahead with their agendas to secure America as a secular republic where all would be free to worship—or not worship—as they saw fit. In their honor and in acknowledgement and appreciation of their effort, members of the Touro Synagogue in Newport, Rhode Island, America's oldest synagogue, read aloud every August a letter addressed to them by George Washington when he was president. He wrote to them in 1790: "All possess alike liberty of conscience and immunity of citizenship . . . [f]or happily the Government of the United States, which gives to bigotry no sanction, to persecution no assistance, requires only that they who live under its protection should demean themselves as good citizens."

In his closing, Washington included a sentiment that applies to Muslims and Christians as well as Jews: "May the children of the Stock of Abraham, who dwell in this land, continue to merit and enjoy the good will of the other inhabitants, while every one shall sit in safety under his own vine and fig tree, and there shall be none to make him afraid." While Adams and Jefferson disagreed strongly with respect to policy, they remained staunchly united on the issue of religious freedom.

Although America's early leaders were exemplars of religious tolerance, and though the First and Fourteenth Amendments to the Constitution guarantee religious freedom and religious civil rights, respectively, attitudes are slow to change. Even in 1960, the Catholic presidential candidate, John F. Kennedy, deemed it necessary to make a speech declaring that his loyalty was to America, not to the pope. And as recently as 2008, during the Republican primary election, the Mormon presidential candidate, Mitt Romney, felt obliged to address misgivings concerning the Church of Latter-day Saints, suspicions that had provoked violence from the time of the church's founding, in the 19th century, when members were massacred by renegade militiamen and its founder, Joseph Smith, and his brother were murdered by a mob. Almost as tragic was that no one was ever convicted of the crime. Anti-Semitism has also been an issue in the United States since colonial times. It was practiced institutionally for decades, and some would argue that it is still practiced, socially, to a certain extent.

Nevertheless, as Davis asserts, America can still be the nation that James Madison envisioned in 1785: "an Asylum to the persecuted and oppressed of every Nation and Religion." "But," Davis maintains, "recognizing that deep religious discord has been part of America's social DNA is a healthy and necessary step. When we acknowledge that dark past, perhaps the nation will return to that 'promised . . . lustre' of which Madison so grandiloquently wrote."

The phrase to which Davis was alluding, "promised . . . lustre," comes from a statement that James Madison uttered in an eloquent argument made in 1784 in favor of the policy, included as Article VI in the Constitution, that excluded religious tests for those seeking public office or, by extension, for voting—"that generous policy, which, offering an Asylum to the persecuted and oppressed of every Nation and Religion, promised lustre to our country."

That legislation was by no means insignificant. According to the late William Miller, the historian and ethicist who taught for many years at the University of Virginia and the author of *The Business of May Next: James Madison and the Founding*, this policy was one of the most symbolic "opinions," as Thomas Jefferson referred to them, that the protectors of freedom made explicit in the First Amendment to the Constitution. Miller explains that "Christianity was cut free from all formal collective support in a way that in Europe it had not known since the Emperor Constantine raised the banner of the cross as the insignia of the Roman state." This was not a small matter with respect to the history of Western civilization. Indeed, he remarks, "there are those who find the separation of church and state, as it would one day come to be called, the most significant of all the departures and novelties in the arrangements of the new nation." That the law would not require that one profess any religion in order to become a legislator, a president, or even a notary public, that no religious profession was necessary in order for one to hold public office or to become a citizen or to vote, was an extraordinary achievement. In fact, such tests had been required throughout Western history, and all the American colonies had at one time or another mandated them, excluding Jews from office virtually everywhere and also excluding Catholics, Quakers, Unitarians, and, certainly, atheists, agnostics, and "free thinkers."

Examining the actual and symbolic meanings of the prohibition of religious tests, Professor Miller concludes that this ruling played a significant role in the decisions made by Europeans—from virtually every country—in the 19th and early 20th centuries to make the challenging journey across the Atlantic in order to put down roots in the new "Empire of Liberty," in Thomas Jefferson's phrase.

Closer to our time, another major development that would influence the progression of interfaith relations in the United States was the Immigration and Nationality Act of 1965, which removed the national-origins quota system that had forged American immigration policy since its establishment, in 1924.

The national quota system limited the number of people who could emigrate from each country, disproportionately favoring Western Europeans, with 70 percent of all immigration slots designated for individuals from three countries: the United Kingdom, Ireland, and Germany. With the creation of the Immigration and Nationality Act, in 1965, all that changed.

The new law replaced the old nationality criteria with an emphasis on family reunification and employment needs, bringing a large wave of immigrants from Asia—many of whom were Hindus, Muslims, and Buddhists, and some were from other religions—and from Latin America. As Beth Katz, founder and executive director of Project Interfaith, acknowledges in her article entitled "Interfaith Relations: 5 Defining Events" (an online article that appeared on the website Omaha.net), the Immigration and Nationality Act is often credited as one of the key reasons why the United States has become the most religiously diverse nation in the world.

CHAPTER 9

Recognizing the Self in All

All things share the same breath—the beast, the tree, the man. . . .
The air shares its spirit with all the life it supports.

~ Chief Seattle,
leader of the Suquamish and Duwamish tribes

In 1967, Swami Satchidananda was among the new immigrants whose exotic garb, customs, and cuisines would add color and spice to the so-called melting pot of American culture. He arrived in New York City on May 24, 1967, and, according to an article in the *Village Voice*, he "came through customs, beaming and radiant. . . ." The wisdom that he accessed through his contact with various spiritual teachers, as well as his own experiences, enlivened him and illuminated the lives of those who came to learn from him. And come they did: Jews, Christians, Muslims, Hindus, Buddhists, agnostics, the "spiritual but not religious" (SBNR)—to use a current designation—and others, all seeking peace and harmony in a world of divisiveness and discord, a world where the unaware often perpetrate violence on those whom they perceive as "other." They flocked to hear Gurudev speak about a different perception of reality, a perception grounded in the knowledge and in the experience that all beings are interconnected, that in the realm of the ultimate reality, we are all one.

"We can see the same spirit in everybody," he taught, "only when we know that we are that spirit, *Atma*, or Self. Only a person who has understood his or her own Self can see that same Self in everybody. Until then, you can never see others in this way. With that spiritual vision, you see that you are not different from anybody else. It is with this understanding that Jesus said, 'I and my Father are one.' Because he, himself, identified with the Holy Spirit, he was able to understand the Holy Spirit."

Gurudev's teachings made such an impact that a few weeks later, on June 10, 1967, he received the Martin Buber Award for Outstanding

Service to Humanity for his work among American youth. In fact, during his five-month stay in New York, before returning to Sri Lanka, not only had he established a team of Yoga teachers whom he had trained to carry on his work, but he had also begun to see his "hippie" devotees transform themselves into a troupe of refined, dedicated spiritual aspirants. He inspired them to develop discipline and a sense of respect, providing them with the basic guidelines for leading a pure and selfless life. He bridged the "generation gap" by fostering understanding between these young people and their parents, and he strongly censured the use of any mind- or mood-altering drugs.

As the classes continued to grow in size, the Integral Yoga Institute once again needed more space. This time the solution was at hand. A large apartment became available right across the hall, thus doubling the size of the IYI. At the same time, a number of the students who had gathered around Gurudev expressed an interest in living at the Institute. They wanted to experience the yogic lifestyle day to day in a supportive environment, and they felt that they needed more guidance. In response, Gurudev told them about traditional *ashram* life; then, he asked them whether they were truly prepared to undertake the self-discipline required to live that type of lifestyle. They all answered in the affirmative.

Happily, the experiment in *ashram* living was a success. Still, while many of the young people were delighted with their new way of life, not everyone felt the same. In fact, some of their parents were upset, especially those who had strong religious connections. They felt that Yoga was taking their children away from them and their traditions. Some even became so distressed that they threatened legal action. Certainly, such fears were understandable, so Gurudev would often converse with those parents and invite them to the IYI to see how their children were living, to see that they were happy, and to gain an understanding of Yoga and its benefits. Many parents came away from those visits with the realization that Yoga may actually help people gain a deeper understanding of their own religion. Also, after their visits, it was not unusual for some parents to take up the study of Yoga.

Others were so irate that they were unwilling to listen to anything that Gurudev had to say. Fortunately, at such times, Gurudev could turn to spiritual leaders like the late Rabbi Joseph Gelberman, who embraced an interfaith perspective and recognized the benefits of Yoga.

Gurudev and Rabbi Gelberman met in 1966. It was Gurudev's first week in New York, and he was invited to participate in an interfaith retreat that was being held in Val Morin, Canada, at the *ashram* of the late Swami Vishnudevananda, who was a brother monk from India and also a disciple of Sri Swami Sivananda's. Rabbi Gelberman, who was already practicing Yoga, was also a speaker at the retreat. As Gurudev tells it, it was a Friday night, and Rabbi Gelberman, who was celebrating the Jewish Sabbath, asked Gurudev to speak. Gurudev, who had never known any Jews in India, thought that the Sabbath was a Christian celebration, so he talked about Jesus Christ and the sacrifice that Jesus had made. After a few minutes, he began to notice that everyone was looking at him in an odd way. As a matter of fact, one of the retreatants became, as Gurudev put it, "ferocious, looking as though he wanted to kill me;" but seeing how calm the rabbi remained, Gurudev thought to himself, "The rabbi must be a great soul." A few months later, when he returned to settle in Manhattan, Gurudev looked up Rabbi Gelberman. They reunited, and the rabbi immediately invited Gurudev and his students to hold their first Hatha Yoga classes at his synagogue.

Rabbi Gelberman, who passed away at age ninety-eight on September 9, 2010, was a warm and jovial man. He was born in Hungary, came to the United States in 1939, immediately joined the military, and was planning to send for his wife and child right before the Second World War broke out in Europe. Tragically, his young wife and small daughter were not able to get out of Europe, and they died during the war. But even personal tragedy didn't diminish Rabbi Gelberman's love of life, his indomitable faith in God and in humanity, and his endearing sense of humor. In fact, both Gurudev and Rabbi Gelberman were known for their ability to convey lofty spiritual teachings with an ample sprinkling of humor.

Rabbi Gelberman, founder of The New Synagogue, taught interfaith concepts in New York City for more than forty years. In 1981, he and Gurudev cofounded the New Seminary, which was the first interfaith seminary in the United States. It was the first seminary devoted to training ministers who would serve people of all faiths. A devout Jew and modern Hasidic rabbi who had a deep love for Jewish traditions and mystical Judaism, Rabbi Gelberman was also a lifelong Yoga practitioner. To explain his interfaith philosophy, he coined the expression "Never instead of, always in addition to." For fifteen years, Swami Satchidananda and Rabbi Gelberman conducted a delightful yearly program titled simply "The Swami and the Rabbi," and the venue chosen for that popular series reflected the scope of their interfaith outlook.

The "Swami and the Rabbi" talk was often held at the Synod House of the Cathedral of St. John the Divine, in Manhattan, the largest Gothic cathedral in the world and a fitting location. Mother of the Episcopal Diocese of New York, the cathedral is famous for its interfaith perspective. Indeed, its 19th-century initiators insisted that it be built as a "house of prayer for all nations," a laudable concept then and even more significant in today's multicultural environment. Their mandate has brought and continues to bring joy to thousands of people from diverse traditions and backgrounds. Religious and secular alike, they come from all over the world to enjoy the annual Feast of Saint Francis, for example, which features the musician Paul Winter's stirring *Missa Gaia* (Earth Mass), with its unique procession of many species of animals, its magnificent modern-dance performance, and its inspiring talks. Since 1985, some 5,000 people—religious leaders, laypeople, parents, and children—along with their pets of all shapes and sizes, flock to the cathedral on the first Sunday of October to join in this marvelous celebration of the Earth. As Paul Winter tells it, he had become aware of the rich diversity of the world's musical traditions, and he felt that the Cathedral of St. John the Divine offered the perfect setting for the multifaceted musical world of the Paul Winter Consort.

Those who had the opportunity to attend the *Missa Gaia* during those times when Gurudev spoke at the cathedral felt as though they were listening to Saint Francis himself. For like that extraordinary patron saint of animals, Gurudev considered all of Earth's creatures brothers and sisters, each a singular expression of the one Source. The following excerpt from one of his talks illustrates this perspective:

The Entire World Is My Family

In essence we are one. We are all related to each other. All we have to do is to understand that and to experience it. We are related in spirit. If we see the spirit in ourselves, we will realize that we are all one. Our true nature is that of a spiritual and divine being. We are essentially spiritual beings made in the image of God. We are all the expressions of God, God multiplied into various forms and names. So, we can say that we are the family of God; we are all sisters and brothers. We are all different colors, sizes, and shapes on the outside, but inside, the same light shines. We may look different, but if we see the spirit, we realize, "I am you; you are me; we are one."

We should rise above all the differences and distinctions and see our spiritual oneness. We should learn to love each other, learn to love everyone equally. We should open our minds and hearts. Even just focusing on this one thought, "I belong to the whole world and the entire world is my family," will make one so happy and peaceful.

Living and working together as one beautiful family with total love is God. Real spiritual experience means moving around with a smiling, loving face. To see the spirit in others and to love everyone, to rise above the differences of the lower nature and bring harmony wherever you are. Ultimately, everyone should love you. Make a resolve: "I will live the kind of life that will make everybody love me, and I will love them." If that happens in your life, you will know that you are growing spiritually.

A real spiritual experience means to see the unity in diversity. See the same spirit in everything. Be gentle, be nice, and be loving. See your own Self in all, and treat everything properly. That is how to show the unity in diversity visibly and powerfully.

Let us know that we are all one in spirit. Essentially, we are one appearing as many. The moment that kind of understanding comes, almost all other problems, both physical and material, will be solved. Anything that is done to bring this knowledge to people is the greatest deed. Any charity that is used for this purpose is the best form of charity. If we work toward real universal love and understanding, then we are going to the very root of other problems. Do what you can for this cause. Learn to care and share, to love and give, and inspire others by your example.

We need to use the spiritual teachings of our chosen faith to help us have real love for one another. It is religion that should help us to understand the spiritual oneness, to make us feel more at home as one family. If there is anyone who separates another individual, saying to that person, "You are different from me," using religion to make that claim, then he or she is not a religious person at all. Thinking about these kinds of situations has made me pray, "God, use me in any way you want. I would like to see that in Your name we become one family." If we want to be happy, we should work for the happiness of all people everywhere. That is the only way to achieve real peace and contentment.

In order to have a better world, we must learn to think of the globe as a whole. Your neighbor is God in a visible form. So, let us have communion with our own neighbors—next door and around the globe. Let us feel that the whole world is our home, that everyone is our brother and sister. It's time to know each other and to live as one global family. To make the world right, each individual should find the ease and peace in their lives. Once you have that peace, others will find many things for you to do to serve the world. Think that you are a nice instrument, ready to be used for the good of all.

Serve one and all. Then you will have served God. Don't even lose a single opportunity to serve others. Serve, serve, serve, and you will find that you also are served. Not everyone can go out and serve physically. Those who have that capacity should do so. Those without that capacity can project their positive thoughts. Those positive suggestions spread all over the globe. Those who have the capacity to do something physical as well should take that opportunity. Mental, physical, material—do something in whatever way you can. That is why all those faculties have been given to you. They are not given just for your own use. Your physical strength, your material wealth, everything is given to you to be used for others. Of course, that doesn't mean that you should not use it for yourself, too, but the major part of it is to be offered to others. That's the way we should mold our lives. We should not think that we are living here for our own sake. We are here for the sake of everyone. On every plane, we should be able to offer ourselves and our possessions for the benefit of humanity and the entire nature.

Prayerful thoughts always bring benefit to people. When ten thousand people feel for a person and pray, all that wishful thinking goes to help him or her. Good thoughts and feelings always reach the ones who are really starving for them. Those who deserve that good thinking will receive it. We simply spread the seeds. When people know that so many others are praying for them, that gives them strength. There is a benefit right away: "Oh, so many people are praying for me. All their good thinking is on my side."

My prayer is always that universal love will light our paths. Every day when you pray, repeat: "May auspiciousness, peace, fullness, prosperity, and happiness be unto all. May all see good in everyone; may all be free from suffering. May the whole world be filled with peace and joy, love and light." When you say this, it shouldn't be just words; you really have to feel it, visualize it. It should be heartfelt when you send your energy out to the world. All prayers will bring benefit, so let us wholeheartedly pray for our world. Let us spend at least a few minutes each day in meditation. To me, those are the most important minutes. These peaceful vibrations will help millions of peace-less minds. Your peaceful vibrations, although you may not even realize their effect, will certainly help many people. You will be helping the whole world to find peace and joy. Let your actions help bring out that cosmic beauty and help to build a better world.

~ from *Integral Yoga Magazine*, Spring 2005

Not only did Gurudev give many talks at the Synod House, but he also became a close friend and colleague of the Very Reverend James Parks Morton, who served for twenty-five years as dean of the cathedral. Upon his retirement, in 1997, Dean Morton founded the Interfaith Center in New York. Like Gurudev and Rabbi Gelberman, and together with them, Dean Morton became well known as an ambassador of interfaith understanding and harmony.

For quite some time, Gurudev was in the United States on a temporary visa, but the members of the New York Integral Yoga Institute were determined to keep him in the country, so they began to inquire about getting him permanent residency status. While visas were given to religious ministers, this particular type of status had never been granted to a foreign clergyperson. The authorities even told Gurudev, "We have been sending religious ministers to other countries, but we have never given a religious minister a permanent visa to this country. Even though there is a provision for that, so far, we have never opened that channel." Apparently, the officials were reluctant to set a precedent.

Even though it seemed that Gurudev would probably be refused the visa, the IYI group persisted until the director of the immigration department agreed to an interview with Gurudev. During the interview, the director asked Gurudev his reason for wanting to stay in the country. Gurudev simply replied, "I have no desire to stay." The director was taken aback. This was the first time in the history of the department that someone applying for a visa had responded in such a way. "What?" he asked. "Do you really mean that?" "Yes, sir," said

Gurudev. "I do mean that." Of course, the director then asked him why he had applied. When Gurudev explained that he was applying because people were asking him to stay, the director responded, "Suppose we say no?" Gurudev told him that it was fine, that in fact they weren't saying no to *him*; they were saying no to the Americans who wanted him to stay. It's between you and them, Gurudev explained, making it clear that he had nothing to lose. At the same time, petitions and letters like the following were pouring into the immigration office:

As a Roman Catholic monk engaged in the study of Eastern religion and philosophy, I want to state that I have known the Swami from the time he came to this country, have had the privilege of discussing with him at length his religious and philosophical views, and am convinced that his presence here in the United States serves a spiritual need felt by representatives of many different religions.

~ Brother David Steindl-Rast, O.S.B.

I have appeared on religious and secular platforms with the Swami and have heard his sermons preached throughout the city. Young people, for whom spiritual, physical, and inspirational guidance previously appeared meaningless and impractical, "come to scoff and remain to pray."

~ Rabbi Joseph Gelberman

The almost two thousand students from Manhattan College and Mount Saint Vincent who attended his lecture here on campus last week did not think they were attending a philosophy lecture or they would not have been there. They were greeting a man who was addressing the spiritual needs of the younger generation. He was saying the same things the Church has been trying to say, but, by saying it to them in a different way and in a different context, he is saying it so they will listen.

~ D. C. H., assistant professor, Department
of Theology, Manhattan College

From the moment I first talked to Swami Satchidananda, I began to realize that he understood my questions and that he could help me find the answers within me and that in him I had found someone who could bring those answers to the surface. I had long ago lost faith in my Protestant upbringing and become an agnostic. The beautiful faith I had in God as a child became more and more distant as I got caught up in the confusion of everyday life. Swami Satchidananda has taught me that God does exist and that He is everywhere if we only take time to stop and look for Him.

~ F. C., Cambridge, Massachusetts

I teach here in the Graduate School of Drama at Yale, and I am a playwright (my play *America Hurrah* is running currently in New York). In both these capacities, as well as personally, I have been greatly enriched by my contact, through his classes, with Swami Satchidananda during the past year. Any true understanding of foreign cultures must come through the authentic work of such inspired and modest men in our midst. On such understanding lies our best hope for a peaceful world.

~ Jean-Claude van Itallie, New Haven, Connecticut

The Swami has been a great inspiration and help, not only to myself but to hundreds more. Such Christ-like figures with genuine words of peace and love have sustained the world from time immemorial. How necessary they are in our own troubled times.

~ J. W., American Book Company, New York

Finally, because of hundreds of letters like these and the dedicated service of those who valued Gurudev's teachings and work, the visa was granted. In fact, that visa was the first ever to be given to a "Minister of Divine Words."

CHAPTER 10

Sharing the Peace

*To truly understand the meaning of compassion
means to understand the interdependence of all living beings.
We are all part of one another.*

~ Thomas Merton, Trappist monk

The IYI continued to grow, and new institutes and centers opened
all over the country. Gurudev continued to live in New York City,
where each Friday evening he gave a talk at the Unitarian Universalist
Church. The New York IYI offered a full schedule of classes, and
teachers conducted special programs outside the Institute, including
classes at the United Nations. Gurudev went wherever there was an
interest and an invitation.

In the spring of 1968, a meeting of individuals representing various
spiritual groups convened in New Hope, Pennsylvania. Gurudev
attended with his friend Rabbi Gelberman. At the end of the
gathering, Gurudev suggested that because all the participants felt so
happy about getting together, maybe they should make it happen more
often. He added, "We will let people know that although we have
superficial differences, if we look deeper, we see that all paths have that
common Source."

Gurudev, Eido Tai Shimano Roshi, a Zen Buddhist monk, and
Brother David Steindl-Rast, a Benedictine monk, got together now
and then. As Brother David explained, "Then Thomas Merton said
that this was something important and asked us to put our meetings
on a more permanent basis. That is how the Center for Spiritual
Studies came about." Its board of directors included Gurudev, Brother
David, Rabbi Gelberman, and Eido Roshi.

The group met once a month, sometimes at the IYI and sometimes
at the Zen Center in New York. Before long, the students of these

spiritual teachers joined in, and it became obvious that the group needed to find a bigger meeting place. As a result, the group created YES, the Yoga Ecumenical Seminary. YES was a retreat site established in Saugerties, New York, slightly less than a two-hour drive from New York City. The site included a twenty-six-room main house, and the expansive grounds even had a secluded waterfall located at the foot of a mountain and surrounded by woods.

According to Gurudev's biography, during the summer months people (at times, several hundred) came together to share an experience, no matter their particular beliefs. Clergy, laity, and students of various faiths participated in a schedule of Hatha Yoga, prayer, meditation, Karma Yoga (selfless service), and *satsang* (spiritual discourse). One summer, twenty students from the Integral Yoga Drug Rehabilitation Program came to participate in the activities. Gurudev, Brother David, Rabbi Gelberman, and Eido Roshi gave lectures and conducted weekend retreats. It was at that time that Gurudev added another innovation: the Yoga Ecumenical Service—now known as the Light Of Truth Universal Service—a groundbreaking interfaith ceremony. (See Appendix 2 for a guide to organizing the Light Of Truth Universal Service.)

Although Christian clergy, seeking to promote greater interdenominational unity among Christians, were engaging in ecumenical dialogue and Christian and Jewish spiritual leaders were meeting to promote greater understanding and cooperation between adherents of those two faiths, there was very little real discourse among clergy of the other world faiths. Effectively, with the Light Of Truth Universal Service, not only did Gurudev lead the way in providing an opportunity for clergy of diverse faiths to discover the commonalities that inform those faiths, but he also made available the unique opportunity for them to experience, firsthand, the essential unity of those faiths. He understood that the religious leaders would take their experience of spiritual unity and cooperation back to their congregations.

In the Light Of Truth Universal Service, representatives of the major faiths and of other known faiths make offerings to a central light, a symbol of the divine light of all faiths. The celebrants, wearing traditional clerical or other garb denoting their faiths, enter slowly and reverently, beginning with the representative of the youngest faith and proceeding to the oldest, as follows: Native American, African, Sikh, Islamic, Christian, Buddhist, Tao, Shinto, Jewish, and Hindu. The final celebrant represents "other known faiths." Carrying a lit taper, each celebrant walks to the altar and, facing the audience, stands around the central light that symbolizes the Divine. The processional music stops, and a gong is often rung as a signal for the celebrants to light the central candle together. The celebrants then extinguish their individual candles and take their seats. The offerings are prayers, each celebrant reciting a prayer from his or her tradition.

After the last offering, there is a call for a "sign of peace" that the celebrants can offer to one another, such as a handshake or an embrace. Then a gong is rung again as celebrants relight their candles—all from the central light—and begin a recessional accompanied by music.

YES became a sanctuary away from the city, a haven for physical and spiritual rejuvenation. The response was enthusiastic.

Ever the interfaith pioneer, Gurudev also introduced the interfaith *kirtan*. He had always included *kirtan*—the chanting of divine sounds or names and the singing of praises and hymns—as part of the Integral Yoga practice. Music is a universal phenomenon, a marvel common to diverse cultures and spiritual traditions. Throughout the ages, human beings have sought, individually and communally, to experience profound spiritual states through sound vibration. Indeed, for centuries ancient and modern yogis have included *kirtan* as part of their spiritual practice, chanting divine names and praises in Sanskrit, the ancient Indo-European language of India and the language of the Hindu scriptures and classical Indian literature.

A powerful healing practice, chanting calms the nerves, purifies the emotions, heals the body, concentrates the mind, and opens the heart, preparing a practitioner for meditation and the highest spiritual state: communion with the Divine. Generally speaking, *kirtan* engenders an experience and creates an atmosphere of harmony, peace, and bliss.

Kirtan begins with the chanting of the universal mantra *OM*, the source of all other mantras. Not a word, but a sound vibration, *OM* "transcends the barriers of age, race, culture, even species" (see hinduism.about.com) and is believed to be the basic sound of the universe. The *Integral Yoga Kirtan* opens with the chanting of this cosmic syllable and continues with prayers that invoke the presence and guidance of the Cosmic Consciousness.

Gurudev described the universality and the benefits of chanting as follows:

> Almost every spiritual tradition practices some form of *kirtan* and mantra *japa*, chanting and repetition of a mantra. At Mount Athos, I saw Greek Orthodox monks holding the rosary and repeating the mantra "Lord have mercy on me." In Tibet, I heard all the Tibetan Buddhist monks chanting "*Om Mane Padme Hum.*" All religions have this practice. It is an important practice that all spiritual seekers can do.

> Practices like *kirtan* can help us to quiet the mind. The goal of Yoga and all spiritual practices in every tradition is to quiet the mind. When the mind is quiet, then you will see yourself as peace, as bliss absolute. The ultimate goal is supreme peace.

> In this modern age, filled with so much chaos, distraction, stress, and busyness, *kirtan* is one of the simplest and easiest spiritual practices. Chanting is really enchanting. Use any name, form, or aspect of the Divine. Use an uplifting thought. Sing, "I love all. I love all. I love all." "Peace for all. Peace for all. Joy for all. Joy for all." Utilize any phrase that makes your mind more elevated, broadened. You know the maxim, "As you think, so you become." We are all thinking beings. We become what we are thinking, so that is why we say to repeat mantras, the various names of God, and uplifting phrases.

> When we talk about God, it is not a person or a particular image. In *kirtan* and in our meditation, we focus on the attributes of God—attributes like compassion, peace, joy, love. Don't we say that God is all blissful, all peaceful, all loving? So

when we think of God, we are thinking of loving all, loving all, loving all. And, ultimately, we will begin to love all. When we are chanting, we can't hate or deny anybody in this world. When we chant, the mind expands and becomes one with everything.

In the 1980s, Gurudev expanded the *Integral Yoga Kirtan* to include a series of chants utilizing divine names from the world's faiths. This *kirtan* was, perhaps, the first interfaith *kirtan* of its kind developed in the United States, and it is sung at Satchidananda Ashram every Saturday evening at *satsang*, during celebrations, and at Integral Yoga centers around the world.*

In the summer of 1970, the IYI sponsored another new event, the first ten-day retreat: ten days of Hatha Yoga, meditation and lectures, vegetarian cuisine, an interfaith worship service, and—most significantly—a coming together in silence. This experience was new for most people, including the students who came to the IYI. They emerged from various backgrounds and lifestyles; they were new to Yoga; and they knew little about the full range of its teachings and practices. They were acquainted with Gurudev only from seeing his picture on the wall. Later on in the 1970s, similar retreats became popular and were offered by many spiritual groups around the United States, but in 1970 the phenomenon was new. How exciting it must have been for staff and participants alike when 250 eager retreatants found their way to the campus of Annhurst College, in Woodstock, Connecticut, the site rented for the event!

At the same time, some participants felt, understandably, a little anxious. They didn't know what to expect. Staff members felt anxious for the same reason and also because they were taking on a large responsibility. In fact, the nuns who ran the college were filled with misgivings; most of their doubts had to do with Yoga. They worried

---

*On June 7, 2014, in honor of Gurudev's 100th birthday and of his interfaith service, the world's first "Interfaith Kirtan for World Peace" was held at the Cathedral of St. John the Divine, bringing together devotional chants from the various world faiths.

whether Yoga was another religion. Was it wrong to allow a Yoga retreat to be held at a college devoted to Christian teachings? It was Brother David, a Catholic monk himself, who allayed their fears; indeed, Brother David had made the arrangements for the retreat to be held at the college. He also persuaded Father George Maloney, a Jesuit priest from Fordham University, to take part in the retreat. It seems that after speaking with Brother David, the sisters were somewhat reassured, although, they were still a bit uncertain. The uncertainties they felt had to do with the retreatants themselves. Would the campus be overrun with droves of undisciplined young people? Hippies perhaps? And would the behavior of these youngsters prove to be uncontrollable and destructive?

When the buses drove in and deposited their passengers, the sisters looked at the young people, casually dressed, some with flowers in their hair, and they also saw that many were older, some even gray-haired and distinguished looking. Though it was still difficult for the nuns to determine what they might expect, happily their fears were quieted during the retreat.

For ten days, in full silence, the retreatants participated in the Yoga practices and listened to talks about Yoga and about the teachings of the various faiths represented by the presenters. The participants also practiced selfless service, contributing to the maintenance of the college grounds. The nuns were pleasantly surprised. Peace reigned. One retreatant described the experience like this:

> After a few days of ups and downs, things began to get better for me. I began to feel more relaxed with the schedule, with my own mind, and with what these different teachers were saying about selflessness and leading a spiritual life. I began to feel a lot lighter, and I noticed that the whole vibration of the retreat seemed to get lighter, too. For the first few days, the retreat had seemed endless; by the last day, I wanted it to go on forever. I vowed that when I got home, I would not lose what I had found there.

On the last morning, everyone gathered in the meeting hall. The silent period had officially ended, but the group had remained silent. Among them were many of the nuns who were on the college staff. It seems that during the ten days, the sisters had gradually begun to attend the talks, and some had even taken Hatha Yoga classes.

Gurudev began the final session by introducing a special guest, his close friend Padma Vibhushan C. V. Narasimhan, who was under-secretary-general of the United Nations. Mr. Narasimhan led the group in a traditional Indian song. Afterward, Gurudev introduced his fellow teachers: Brother David, Rabbi Gelberman, and Father Maloney. Each spoke about his own experience of the retreat. Gurudev also invited the mother superior of the college to speak. She told of her early fears about the retreat, confessed that they had been dissolved, and complimented the retreatants on their beauty and self-discipline, letting them know that they would be welcome again. With her arms opened wide in a gesture of embrace, she concluded by saying, "*OM Shanti, OM Shanti, OM Shanti OM* [*OM* Peace, Peace, Peace]."

The first silent retreat proved to be a great success. It provided an ideal environment for people of all ages and different walks of life to discover the spiritual knowledge within their own psyches and to explore how that knowledge is reflected in the fundamental principles of the various spiritual paths. The program also highlighted Gurudev's interfaith teachings and service, and, in a sense, it prefigured the physical manifestation of a concept he had envisioned since the 1950s: an actual place that would be dedicated to all faiths, a site where people from different religions could come together under one roof to pray and meditate in silence.

Like the sages of old, Gurudev understood that world peace would be possible only when people loved their neighbors as they loved themselves. Before that could happen, they had to love themselves. He also knew that self-love emerged from self-understanding. He taught and embraced the ancient Delphic maxim, set forth in both Eastern and Western philosophy, that the fundamental goal of life is to "know thyself."

How to Know Your Self

The aim of all spiritual practices is to know your real Self, to know the Knower. The Bible says, "Love your neighbor as yourself." But without knowing what your Self is, how can you love your Self in him or her? Know your Self and, then, see your own Self in your neighbor's Self. Then, you can love him or her as your Self. To love everybody or everything as the spirit, you should realize your spiritual truth; you should realize the God in you.

Actually, have you ever seen yourself, even your physical self? Have you ever seen your face? Only in a mirror, isn't that so? But suppose I broke the mirror; could you still see your face? No. But would you have lost it then? No. What you see in a mirror is the image, not the original.

Moreover, if you look for your true nature in a distorted mirror, you will see a crooked face. But is your face really crooked? So, what is the mirror in this analogy? The mirror is your mind. And to see your true Self, you must have a clean, clear, calm mind. Some people keep the mirror clean and realize that they are beautiful. Others, unfortunately, don't dust it well. Some even break it, and some bend it. But when you make the mind calm and serene, you realize that the soul and God are one and the same, without any distortions, without any color. Furthermore, the body, also, should acquire that serenity that is called the relaxed or pure state. A very healthy and relaxed body together with a calm and serene mind will allow the true light, or the true nature of the Self within to express itself without any distortion.

Primarily, though, one should take care of the mind, because the body is only an instrument of the mind. Normally, we identify ourselves as a mind and a body. That's why we call ourselves by different names and seem to differ from each other. But the variations and definitions come only when we identify with the body and mind.

By nature we are at ease and in peace. However, due to negligence or efforts aimed at satisfying the selfish desires of the senses, we disturb that ease and peace. And when we disturb the ease, we feel *dis-eased*. We were fine originally, and, then, we lost that fine-ness. That's when we became *defined*. Unfortunately, the moment we define ourselves—or limit the Self—we are no longer fine. That's why all the scriptures, all the sages, saints and prophets tell us to stop defining. This is the process of re-*finement*. This is the essence of all Yoga and all scriptures.

~ Swami Satchidananda, from *Pathways to Peace*

When we consider that the Integral Yoga retreat provides an environment fostering a greater awareness of the nature of consciousness, a deeper understanding of the universal truths that link the various spiritual traditions, and a heightened perception of the unity of spirit that underlies the diversity of creation, we become aware of the efficacy and brilliance of such an approach. The group meditation and Hatha Yoga practices, a healthful, balanced diet, inspiring lectures, nature walks, silence, and the harmonious vibration during the retreat all serve to create a microcosm of peace—a miniature heaven on Earth.

Speaking of a heaven on Earth, in New York City many people were drawn to the Integral Yoga Institute, which had become a sanctuary from the frenetic energy and stress of city life. The Institute grew so rapidly that the members began looking for a second location. They soon found a wonderful, six-story building downtown, on West 13th Street, in the heart of Greenwich Village.

The dedication of the second Integral Yoga Institute took place on October 15, 1970, and on October 16th Gurudev began a six-month tour of Europe (in Rome, he met for the second time with His Holiness Pope Paul VI), India, Malaysia, Singapore, Hong Kong, Japan, the Philippines, Australia, New Zealand, Fiji, and Hawaii. When he returned to America after his world tour, he shared a dream, a vision that he hadn't disclosed before. It wasn't a new vision; it had come to him a long time before, though he hadn't expressed it to his American students. It was the vision of a community founded on yogic principles, where people from all walks of life could come to live and work together in harmony for the good of all. It wouldn't be a community created only for members of the IYI or for Americans. It would be a model community for the whole world, inspiring others to create similar communities, following whatever spiritual teachings they preferred. He described this model community as a "Yoga village," or "Yogaville."

Gurudev's vision, as well as the name Yogaville, resonated with the students, sparking their enthusiasm. How unique: a community founded on the principles and practices of Yoga, where people of different faiths could explore the similarities and differences between those faiths through open and honest communication and where misunderstandings and misinterpretations could be acknowledged and, hopefully, rectified. As Gurudev explains it in the following excerpt, right knowledge can dispel hatred and violence and replace them with love and peace.

Religion Doesn't Preach Hatred and Killing

Now, more than ever, we must understand that the purpose of religion is not to separate us. True faiths don't preach hatred and killing, nor did any of the prophets. It's the people who wrongly interpret the scriptures who create the divisions.

Division comes if we put our egos into the teachings of these religions. Let us strive to be free of that kind of egoism. Some terrorists say they do these terrible acts for God and in the name of God. God did not ask them to do this. Even the scriptures, the words of sages and saints, are understood through one's own mind. We interpret everything the way we want, depending on the state of our minds. Allah or Muhammad or Jesus or Moses or Shankara never recommended this kind of violence. Even when they used different words, they taught, "Love your neighbor as yourself."

However, some people wrongly interpret the scriptures in distorted ways. Here is a story to illustrate this point:

Once upon a time, there was a condemned prisoner who had been sentenced to death and was about to be hanged. Right at that moment, a message came to the authorities in the form of a telegram. Unfortunately, there was no punctuation in the telegram.

One of the authorities read: "HANG HIM. NOT LET HIM GO." Another one of the authorities, someone who had a kind heart and felt sorry for this man, said: "We are ready to hang him already; why should they have sent such a message? There is something wrong with that. Let me read it."

He read the telegram like this: "HANG HIM NOT. LET HIM GO."

Each person read the same message from his own perspective. And that is how "interpretation" occurs. And, that is why we have "Holy" Crusades and Jihad. In the name of God, some individuals wrongly interpret scriptures as saying, "Kill people." No. God didn't want it, and the sages and saints who gave the teachings never wanted it. If people want to do something evil, they can always quote scriptures as their authority.

~ Swami Satchidananda, from *Adversity & Awakening*

The idea of a Yoga community dedicated to the principles of nonviolence and a healthy lifestyle and open to people from all the different faith traditions appealed to many of the devotees. Donations began to pour in, in amounts both large and small. One enthusiastic couple, both teachers, donated several thousand dollars from their pooled income. Another donor, Sister Agnes Therese, a Catholic nun from Kansas who had attended the Annhurst retreat, contributed $1.00 a month from her $10.00 monthly allowance. Children donated pennies.

Despite the great enthusiasm, however, many difficulties arose. Finding a place both affordable and suitable, for example, presented a challenge. Although more than a year had passed, during his many travels, Gurudev continued to talk about Yogaville as a community that would serve as a model of cooperative living.

Only in 1972, a year and a half after Gurudev had revealed his vision, did the group find the perfect location with the perfect price, in a rural northeastern area of Connecticut. Everyone loved the property, a lovely fifty-eight-acre wooded estate in Pomfret Center. The estate included a solidly built fifty-room house constructed in the beginning of the 20th century and an adjacent building where classes and lectures could be held. By chance, it was only a few miles from Annhurst College, where, by this time, the IYI had conducted two ten-day silent interfaith retreats.

The dedication of Satchidananda Ashram–Yogaville took place on April 14, 1973. Gurudev spoke of it this way:

> Yogaville is an abode of perfect dedication—an inspiration to express the True Self; an embrace to all nations, cultures, and creeds; a community expressing the unity in diversity through a life of purity and serenity; a model world of health and harmony, peace and prosperity; a spiritual center for study, research, and growth. Let us walk together, talk together, live together, love together.

Swami Satchidananda (standing) on the banks of the Ganges River with his Guru, Sri Swami Sivananda.

(below) Buddhist bhikku Sri Ananda Maitreya (far right) and his students, with Swami Satchidananda, Sri Lanka.

(above) Swami Satchidananda visiting Mount Athos, Greece, 1966.

(below) Swami Satchidananda teaching a Yoga class during "East–West: One Heart," an interfaith program at Princeton University, New Jersey, sponsored by the Catholic Art Association, 1969.

*(above) A private audience with His Holiness Pope Paul VI
at the Vatican, 1966.*

*(below) Swami Satchidananda with His Holiness Pope John Paul II
(now Saint John Paul II), Rome, 1984.*

(above) In Sri Lanka, Swami Satchidananda (far left) is inspired to organize the first interfaith Guru Poornima, with photos of spiritual masters from various faiths represented, 1953.

(below, l-r) Sixteen years later, he cofounds an interfaith organization, the Center for Spiritual Studies, with Rabbi Joseph Gelberman (far left), Brother David Steindl-Rast (far right), and Eido Tai Shimano Roshi (not pictured), 1969.

The first Integral Yoga interfaith retreat is held at Annhurst College, South Woodstock, Connecticut, 1970:
(above) Yoga Ecumenical Service (later renamed the Light Of Truth Universal Service).

(below, l-r) Father George Maloney, Rabbi Joseph Gelberman, Swami Satchidananda, Brother David Steindl-Rast.

(above) Temple of Understanding Advisory Board meeting, New York, early 1980s. Founded in 1960 by Juliet Hollister, over the years its work has been supported by leading interfaith advocates. (l-r) Swami Satchidananda, Dr. Karan Singh, Father Thomas Keating, Dr. Robert Muller.

(below) "Word Out of Silence" Symposium is held at Mt. Saviour Monastery in Elmira, New York, 1972: (l-r) Sister Jose, unknown participant, Rev. Josu Sazaki Roshi, Ram Dass, Stephen Durkee (later, Shaykh Nooruddeen), Swami Satchidananda, Father Raimon Panikkar, Father Basil Pennington.

(above) Yoga Ecumenical Service at Satchidananda Ashram-Yogaville East, Connecticut, 1977: (clockwise from right) Taj Inayat Khan, Prabhasa Dharma Roshi (Gesshin), Rabbi Joseph Gelberman, Swami Satchidananda, Brother David Steindl-Rast, Father Robert Beh.

(below) Conference on Nuclear Disarmament, Stanford University, 1982, sponsored by the Meeting of the Ways: (l-r) Ram Dass, Ken Keyes, Dr. Ramamurti Mishra, unnamed student of Yogi Bhajan, unnamed Native American representative, Swami Satchidananda, Daniel Berrigan, Yogi Bhajan.

(above) International Press Conference for Religious Peace, sponsored by the Embrace Foundation and the Sufi Order, at the United Nations chapel, 1985.

(below) Interfaith service marking opening of 54th session of UN General Assembly: (from far left) Rev. James P. Morton; Secretary-General Kofi Annan; H. E. Theo Ben-Gurirab, prime minister of Namibia; Sri Chinmoy (3rd to right of the prime minister); Swami Satchidananda (4th from near right), 1999.

(above) A playful interfaith moment with Buddhist monk, France, early 1980s.

(below) Swami Satchidananda and Rev. James P. Morton with baby porcupines and an elephant during the St. Francis Feast Day procession of animals, Cathedral of St. John the Divine, 1986.

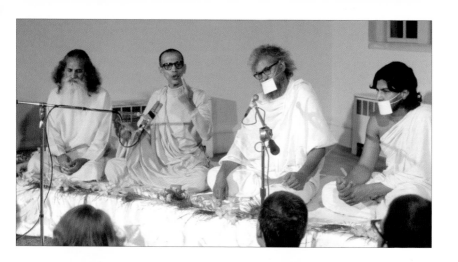

(above) Hindu-Jain program at Satchidananda Ashram-Yogaville, Connecticut, late 1970s: (l-r) Swami Satchidananda, Swami Chidananda, Jain monk Muni Sushil Kumari, and an unnamed Jain monk.

(below) Swami Satchidananda at Shantivanam Ashram in rural South India, with Father Bede Griffiths (Swami Dayananda) and the "meditating Jesus," a statue that Fr. Bede designed, early 1980s.

(above) Swami Satchidananda with his "non-believer" interpreter and Russian Orthodox monks in a prayer circle, Leningrad, 1986.

(below) Interfaith service organized by Swami Satchidananda's students to close the 1988 Soviet-American Citizens' Summit Washington, D.C.: (l-r) unnamed; Fr. Luis Dolan; Swami Satchidananda; Sergei Petrov, Russian Orthodox metropolitan filaret of Odessa; unnamed representatives of the Islamic faith; Rabbi Yuri A. Korzhenevich; Rama Jyoti Vernon.

(above) Symposium organized by Thanks-Giving Foundation in honor of the 20th anniversary of Nostra Aetate, 1985: (l-r) Buddhist monk (not pictured), Cardinal Arinze, Swami Satchidananda, Dr. Fred Streng, Rabbi Jordon Ofseyer, Dr. Muzammil Siddiqi.

(below) Swami Satchidananda, Queen Noor of Jordan, Rev. James P. Morton receive, in its inaugural year, the Juliet Hollister Award for their interfaith and humanitarian service, United Nations, 1994.

Parliament of the World's Religions, Chicago, Illinois, 1993:
(above) A Buddhist monk from Vietnam requests a photo with Swami Satchidananda to
commemorate this historic occasion of the centennial anniversary of the first parliament in 1893.

(below) Swami Satchidananda and the Dalai Lama collaborate, together and with other
dignitaries, on the creation of a "Declaration Toward a Global Ethic." This document was signed
by more than two hundred leaders from over forty faith traditions.

(above) Interreligious Friendship Group planning session with
President Jimmy Carter at the Carter Center, Atlanta, Georgia, 1999.

(below) Temple of Understanding delegation at the White House with
President George H. W. Bush during the signing of the 1990 Thanksgiving Day
proclamation: (l-r) Buddhist representative, Rabbi Jordon Ofseyer, President Bush,
unnamed, Swami Satchidananda, Juliet Hollister, Dr. Mohammed Abdul Raouf.

(above) Partial view of the upper sanctuary of the Light Of Truth Universal Shrine (LOTUS). A central light rises and splits into rays illuminating the altars of each faith.

(below) LOTUS honorary advisory council members and other dignataries, representing many religious traditions, join Swami Satchidananda for the World Faiths Symposium held at the Martin Luther King, Jr. Performing Arts Center, Charlottesville, Virginia, just prior to the LOTUS dedication, 1986.

The LOTUS illuminated during special festivities.

CHAPTER 11

Undoism

People often ask me, "What religion are you?
You talk about the Bible, the Koran, the Torah. Are you a Hindu?"
I say, "I am not a Catholic, a Buddhist, or a Hindu but an undo.
My religion is undoism. We have done enough damage.
We have to stop doing any more
and simply undo the damage we have already done."

~ Swami Satchidananda, from *Beyond Words*

During the almost two years of planning and effort that it took
to transform the estate in Pomfret into a community, some of the
students who had been with Gurudev for several years had begun to
think of making a deeper commitment. They were thinking seriously
about dedicating themselves, as Gurudev had, to a life of spiritual
service. In response to their interest, Gurudev began to speak to them
about renunciation. He spoke cautiously, though, knowing that the
concept was not easy to understand and that the commitment was
difficult to make. When he saw that the interested students really
wanted to make such a commitment, that they were ready to renounce
everything that one calls "mine" and take monastic vows, he agreed to
initiate them into pre-*sannyas*. Pre-*sannyas*, the stage before becoming
a *sannyasin*, an ordained monk, offers the initiate the opportunity to
discover whether the path of total renunciation is the right one for
him or her.

Some of the students were concerned because they did not feel
drawn to the monastic life and wondered whether it was only by
taking monastic vows that they could serve fully or demonstrate their
commitment. Gurudev assured them that "from the point of view of
spiritual attainment, it makes no difference." "The only difference,"
he explained, "is that a renunciate is freer to serve. A householder has
to think of his or her family obligations first; a renunciate can just go

and serve wherever needed. But don't forget that many great saints were also householders. It is not the form but the dedication that is important."

In February 1973, Gurudev initiated the first group, consisting of fourteen devotees, into pre-*sannyas*.

As the *sannyas* and *ashram* traditions originated in India and are grounded in Hinduism, it is not surprising that visitors often posed such questions as "Are the swamis here Hindu monks?" and "Is this a Hindu *ashram*?" Typically, Gurudev would reply in this way:

> They are dressed like Hindu monks. We do something that the Hindus do, but, essentially, the swamis and the *ashram* follow the religion of undoism. They are undo monks. That's why they don't do anything here. [*Lots of laughter.*] Actually, they do serve in various ways, and they teach. What I mean by saying that our religion is undoism is that because we have done enough damage to humanity and to nature in the name of religion and God, it's now time to undo all that. We have done enough damage. Look at history. Countless people killed in the name of race and religion, God and religion. More than even natural calamities, it's our stupidity that has killed so many people.
>
> You may call it anything—Hindu or undo or Christian or Buddhist or Jewish or Muslim or no religion—but our religion is the basic foundation of all the religions, all the faiths. What we practice is found in every faith, in every religion. That means we want to be good and do good. That's our religion. *We are be-gooders and do-gooders.* We want our lives to be easeful and peaceful so that we can be useful. That's our religion. You can label it any way.
>
> You may ask, "Then why do the swamis wear orange?" They wear this color to show that they are dedicated people ready to serve you. It's a badge. When you see a swami, you know that he or she is a public servant. Selfless service is their motto. You can ask them for any kind of help. If they can help

you, they will do it. To show the world that they are dedicated people, they have to have some sign. So, each community has a different costume to show that. We picked this custom up from the Hindu religion.*

~ Sri Swami Satchidananda, from a talk
given on October 22, 1994

Again and again, Gurudev referred to this spiritual approach as "undoism." He characterized this system as the foundation of all the religions, drawing a parallel with the teachings of Yoga. "What we practice," he explained "is found in every faith, in every religion." One aims to be good and to do good and to live a peaceful, useful life. Moreover, Gurudev's "undoism" never asks anyone to give up his or her chosen religion. When asked whether his students had to do so, he would reply as he did in this excerpt from a talk included in his small book *Heaven on Earth*:

No. Never, never, never. We don't believe in that kind of conversion. Just because I love my mother, should I ask you to renounce your mother and love my mother? I should know that as I love my mother, you also love your mother. So we say, "Let us each love our mothers." There is no need to give up your own mother. In fact, you should not do that. Be loyal to your parents, your religion, your country; but, at the same time, love the other fellow's also. That's why it is a universal approach. It is not uniformity, but universality—unity in diversity. We are not trying to put everything into one religion.

The world is really beginning to understand this now. There are many, many global interfaith conferences. The time has come; the world has shrunk. We cannot separate ourselves and deny each other. It's time to know, respect, and love one another and to live as one global family.

---

*Orange also symbolizes material renunciation and is said to bring peace and tranquility to the mind.

Throughout the 1970s, Gurudev traveled continually all over the United States and abroad, answering invitations to share the yogic teachings and his unique spiritual approach. Many of his students had supposed that he would remain in one place now that they had an *ashram*, but more and more people began looking to him for spiritual guidance and interfaith understanding, and the invitations kept arriving.

Gurudev became known and respected the world over as a dynamic spiritual leader, an ardent teacher and proponent of Yoga, a staunch supporter of interfaith harmony, and an apostle of peace. His interfaith service included talks at the annual Yoga Ecumenical Seminars (YES) and the "Swami and Rabbi" annual programs; the Mount Saviour Monastery "Word Out of Silence" Symposium with talks by Alan Watts, Father Raimon Panikkar, Pir Vilayat Khan, among others; a ten-day interfaith silent retreat in Monticello, New York, with Sant Keshavadas (founder of the Temple of Cosmic Religion), Rabbi Gelberman, Rabbi Shlomo Carlebach (the "singing rabbi"), Ram Dass, and Brother David; the Meeting of the Ways Ecumenical Conference; the State of Brotherhood Ecumenical Symposium in Oregon; and the Annhurst III Integral Yoga Retreat with Brother David, the Korean Zen master Seung Sahn, Rabbi Gendler, André Van Lysebeth from Belgium, and Sri N. Mahalingham from India.

These programs and others like them inspired thousands of people, exposing them to spiritual traditions other than their own and fostering an appreciation of those traditions. Father Richard B. Griffin, a Roman Catholic priest and retired chaplain of Harvard University, wrote about his "Word Out of Silence" experience on his blog:

> Until middle age, I had never known anyone who was not either a Christian or a Jew. Muslims, Buddhists, Hindus and people espousing the other religious traditions of the world simply did not come across my suburban paths during childhood and adolescence. And obviously all of my colleagues in the Jesuit order where I lived in early adulthood shared my own Christian faith.

In 1972, however, I took part in what was billed as "Word Out of Silence: Spiritual Formation East and West," a symposium held at Mount Saviour Monastery in Elmira, New York. There the Benedictine monks hosted religious leaders from a dozen different traditions in a week of prayer and other spiritual exercises. It meant my first exposure to turbaned swamis and Zen masters with shaved heads, an experience that helped to change my world view.

I will always remember the strain in my leg muscles as I assumed the lotus position for meditation each morning at 4:30 under the direction of a Japanese roshi. Though I was used to my own strict religious discipline, I worried about being able to last out the week under that austere regimen.

At that time, only in the middle of my life journey, old age did not interest me as a subject for reflection. I was still too young for thoughts of later life to impinge upon my consciousness. Though I did often contemplate the thought of my own death, that event seemed far off in the future.

Thirty years later, however, I have become intent on finding whatever light on old age is offered by the various religious traditions of the world. Surely their wisdom, preserved for thousands of years, must have something important to say about what it means to grow old. And they must speak to the end of life on earth and its meaning for the future.

During this decade, Gurudev met Peter Stewart, the founder of Thanks-Giving, headquartered in Dallas, Texas, and consisting of the National Thanks-Giving Commission and Thanks-Giving Square, a park operated by the nonprofit Thanks-Giving Foundation, which has been doing seminal work in the interfaith field since 1964.

In 1970, the planners of the park asked Gurudev for his advice in the designing of the universal meditation room to be built in the square. The celebrated architect Philip Johnson designed the park, which was dedicated in 1976 to promote the idea of giving thanks as a universal human value. At its entrance, visitors encounter the Court of All Nations and the Wall of Praise, which incorporates a portion of the text from Psalm 100, the New Testament psalm for expressing gratitude, and a mosaic based on Norman Rockwell's painting *The Golden Rule*. Visitors are led from the Wall of Praise to a fifty-foot bell tower, whose three bronze bells, designed in the form of the Liberty Bell, ring every hour. Next to the bell tower stands the Ring of Thanks and Circle of Giving, a fourteen-foot-diameter ring covered in gold leaf through which a visitor may pass before entering Thanks-Giving Square's courtyard.

The focal point of Thanks-Giving Square is the Chapel of Thanks-Giving, a small, spiral tower that houses an enclave for offering prayerful thanks. The chapel's entrance lies at the end of a bridge that runs over a cascading waterfall. In the chapel is the stained-glass "Glory Window," mounted atop the spiral, whose colors become brighter as the spiral reaches its apex and even brighter as it reaches the center. An etched-glass window, "The Spirit of Thanks-Giving," features a dove over the doorway.

This multifaith organization implements the Multifaith Exploration and Exchange Program, dedicated to interfaith understanding, and tours, presentations, and various programs take place throughout the year.

The foundation initiated yet another innovation in 1982: the Declaration of World Thanksgiving. According to the foundation, "Each signer of this declaration brings a unique depth to the healing vision of gratitude. In this vision, all of the signers stand together in an effort that offers vitality and wholeness for the entire planet. Together, they create a better world, a stronger humanity." Gurudev was invited to sign the declaration in its second year. And up to the year 2000, 228 distinguished people from many religious and cultural backgrounds who regard the qualities of gratitude, praise, and thanksgiving as central to human life signed the Declaration of World Thanksgiving. Each year it was presented to the United Nations, and the tradition continued for several decades.

Also in the 1970s, Gurudev, along with Mother Teresa, Brother David, and other luminaries, took part in the Spiritual Summit Conference in New York, honoring the thirtieth anniversary of the United Nations. He conducted an All-Faith Day celebration at the *ashram*, met with the Dalai Lama, and participated in a five-day program at the University of Notre Dame entitled "Doing Prayer."

Gurudev's biography recounts that "Doing Prayer" was a seminar conducted for 190 Catholic nuns and priests from all over the United States whose mission was to teach other members of the clergy. Each of the five days was devoted to one speaker, who would offer practical experience to the group in a particular form of prayer. Gurudev, the only non-Christian participating in the workshop, had been asked to speak about Eastern prayer.

During the first day, Gurudev took part in the workshop about "image" prayer given by the Reverend Morton Kelsey. Reverend Kelsey described a detailed scene from the life of Jesus, asking the group to visualize the scene. In the discussion that followed, Gurudev commented that this practice reminded him of one often done in India by devotees who live too far away from a holy place of pilgrimage to be able to visit there in person. Those individuals may sit in their own homes and make a pilgrimage mentally. According to Gurudev, if they do so with sincere devotion, they may actually experience *darshan*, or God's presence. It was characteristic of Gurudev to make people aware of the similarities between their various traditions without erasing their unique qualities.

On the second day, Gurudev taught a Hatha Yoga class to more than 150 nuns and priests and also led them in a walking meditation. At their request, he performed a Hindu worship service, a *puja*. During the *puja*, one honors the Divine in the form of light, a statue or an image, or any other preferred object, symbolically offering such items as incense, flower petals, decorations, food, and drink, in much the same way that, in the East, one would customarily treat an esteemed guest.

As usual, Gurudev began the service with Sanskrit prayers and chanting. While performing the *puja*, he quietly explained the meaning of each action. He offered flower petals and waved a camphor light, symbolizing the melting or merging of the ego into the Divine source.

Later, he led the group to lunch. Chanting, they entered the dining room. Everyone took a candle and lit it from the single candle that Gurudev had brought from the altar. The room glowed with candlelight as they followed Gurudev in a prayer of thanksgiving. Having asked him earlier to propose a menu, they enjoyed the vegetarian meal that he had suggested.

The theological leader of the conference, Professor William Storey, thanked Gurudev for the *puja*, which he said he found very moving. He nonetheless felt obliged to confess to a doubt concerning a remark of Gurudev's about eating an apple with the attitude that one is eating God's body; that is to say that one is seeing God in everything. Professor Storey thought he understood that remark but admitted that, for him, "serious distinctions among the kinds of 'presence' of God" exist. He offered as an example that Christ is present in every person (for him a great theological truth) and also present in the Eucharist. As he pointed out, "They are not the same form of presence. The transforming power of God as I understand it, which can take place because of the yielding character of bread and wine, doesn't take place so easily in man because of the unyielding character of flesh and blood. So it's when you get into these distinctions that I start to feel uneasy."

At this point, Professor Storey ended his remarks, because he didn't want to "put a damper" on all the positive statements he had made (and had meant sincerely) about Gurudev's comments. He also asked Gurudev whether he would respond. As recorded in his biography, this was Gurudev's response:

> Well, on the last point, which our Father Storey was a little hesitant to say, I'd like to ask: Is there anything wrong in seeing God's body in an apple? Do we in any way bring God down to a lower level or commit any sin in seeing it like that?

God may not be present in the same way as in the Eucharist. But where is the harm of seeing God there? On the contrary, we are elevating the apple to a higher level. It depends upon your feeling. Not all the people who receive communion see the same way, feel the same way. To be more frank, I have taken communion many times and have watched others who come and take communion. To some of them, it is just a piece of bread. But when I receive it, I feel that I am actually receiving God. So, it's the *bhavana*, as we call it in Sanskrit, the *feeling* behind the action. If you have the right feeling, everything is God's body.

After all, what is Christ? Who is he? Just a body? We say Christ was crucified. What is it that was crucified? Certainly, not Christ. Nobody can touch Christ. Nobody can nail Christ. He is the true spirit of God. It is the body that has been nailed, the body in which Christ lived. When you talk about "Christ being born in you," you mean the spirit. The spirit is always in you, untainted, unaffected by all these things. So, as such, it is the son of God, or God Himself. Every expression is the son of God. An apple is the son of God. We can treat it that way if we can see it that way. We see the Mother Earth. Anything that comes from Mother Earth is mother's milk. It is the essence of Mother. If one doesn't have the faith, then even in the Eucharist—the bread and wine—one may not see anything. Personally, I feel that when I walk on the Earth, I am walking on the breast of my Mother; when I sleep, I feel I am sleeping on Her lap. So there is nothing wrong in seeing everything as Divine. If you treat everything as Divine, it becomes Divine. If you have the faith, you receive the benefit."

When Gurudev finished speaking, one of the priests in the workshop stood up:

I'd like to share something that I've realized during the last few days. I sense that I have not become what I am supposed to be. I don't think that the interest many Christians have in the East is an interest in setting aside our Christian faith. Rather, we see in the holy people of the East a certain awareness. Swami Satchidananda has become who he says we all are. If I, as a Christian, were to become who I say I am, I think I, too, would be able to go beyond the Eucharist to the apple. The real difficulty is that many of us have not really become who we say we are, so we dogmatically think that the apple cannot be God's body. But if we were to become like Saint Francis, for example, what would we see that apple to be? I haven't realized it yet, but I sense that it has to do with what we really are.

Ironically, and probably unbeknownst to him, this self-reflective Christian priest from the West sounded like a true yogi from the East, for the question implicit in his sharing—Who am I?—is the focal point of the branch of Yoga called Jnana Yoga. The Sanskrit word *jnana* means wisdom, and Jnana Yoga is the Yoga of self-knowledge through inquiry, or self-analysis. That was and is the point of Gurudev's "undoistic" approach to spirituality: to lift the veils of dogma and misinterpretations in order to uncover the truth at the heart of each religion. Similarly, the practice of Jnana Yoga enables us to peel away the layers of conditioning and delusions that prevent us from realizing who we really are.

When discussing the nature of religion, Gurudev drew on the literal English translation of the term, "to bind back." To him, the purpose of religion was to return us to the source. The process was one of refinement. In the beginning, as newborns, we are *fine*, but as we grow up, we begin to *de-fine* ourselves. Even though when someone asks us how we are and we say, "I'm fine," we really don't want to stay fine. What we want is to *de-fine* ourselves: I'm a man, she's a woman, he's a teacher, she's a computer analyst, she's smart, he's dumb, I'm black, you're white, they're Sunnis, we're Shiites, I'm Methodist, she's Catholic, he's a Republican, you're a Democrat; and on it goes, *ad infinitum*.

An exceptional storyteller, Gurudev frequently presented scriptural allusions to make a philosophical or theological point. In the anecdote that follows, he employs a well-known scene from the Torah to illustrate that in order to experience our divine God-like nature, we must renounce our attachment to all the identities that we have accumulated during our lifetime:

> When someone asks you how you are, you say, "I am fine." You say that, but you don't mean it. That is the problem. Unconsciously, you say you are fine, but you don't remain fine. You define yourself. But if you took away all your definitions, you'd return to your fineness. You are a refined person. It is as simple as that. So, how do you want to be a refined person? Have no definitions. Simply say, "I am I." That is all.
>
> That is what God said. God is a super-refined person, un-defined, a fine person. And Moses wanted to define God, so when he heard God speaking, he asked, "Who is that talking?"
>
> And God said, "I am."
>
> Moses asked, "What is that? I am who?" He expected to hear, "I am God." Or "I am this" or "I am that." He wanted to hear that. It's almost like somebody knocking on your door. You say, "Who is that?" If that person simply says, "I am," don't you ask, "I am who?" Well, so did Moses. And what was the answer?
>
> "I am that I am."
>
> That is to say, I am fine. I never defined myself, so I am that I am.
>
> If you go to that level, then you are a refined person. You are a religious person. "To bind back" is the meaning of religion. So you can use any method, any name to bring you back to your true nature. It doesn't matter: Christianity, Buddhism, Hinduism, Islam, Judaism, Sikhism, Jainism, or any "ism." Ultimately, all the "isms" should serve to undo the attachment to the definitions. That's why my religion is what? Undoism.
>
> Undo everything. We have done enough damage. Haven't we killed enough people in the name of religion and God? If

you understand the meaning of religion, there is no problem. Hindu religion. Islamic religion. These are all different spiritual paths to reach the one religion that has many expressions. The Hindu scriptures put it this way:

Ekam sat vipraha bahudha vadanti.
Truth is one. Sages express it in many ways.

The ancient sages realized this, and when they had to use their words to tell others what they realized, they used their own languages. They expressed their realization in different ways, but the realization is one. When you begin to express it, you have to use your mind, and minds are different. Not all the minds communicate in the same language.

So that is the essence of religion. If you realize that, you are a realized person.

But, how do you go about that? By seeing all as God personified. Everything. Everything. Not only people, but all things. The scientists put it clearly. In scientific terms, what is everything? All is nothing but a bunch of atoms, a big mass of atoms, appearing as people, as this light, this floor, this ceiling. Whatever you see, and all you don't see, the entire universe is filled with atoms. Even in between what you see and don't see, there is a space, and that space is also filled with atoms. Therefore, that means that the atom is God. It's omnipresent, they say. And it's omniscient and omnipotent. So, if you realize that *Omni*, then there is no problem.

~ Swami Satchidananda, from a talk given on June 23, 1996

According to Gurudev, Yoga itself can be characterized as undoism because its techniques enable us to undo the patterns of thinking and acting that disturb the mind, limiting our capacity to experience our true nature. In the *Yoga Sutras*, the text in which the ancient sage Patanjali presents a systematic exposition of the teachings and practices of Yoga, the second *sutra* (the word is Sanskrit for thread), or aphorism, defines Yoga as *yogas chitta vritti nirodhah*: Yoga is the settling of or the restraint of the modifications of the mind. In other words, Yoga is peace of mind. And when the mind becomes calm, it becomes clear, revealing the essential unity underlying the teachings of the various faiths. That is the message that Gurudev conveyed to audiences all over the world:

> There is one Cosmic Essence, all-pervading, all-knowing, all-powerful. This nameless, formless essence can be approached by any name, any form, any symbol that suits the individual. That is why we have all the religions. But we should never forget our essential unity.

CHAPTER 12

A Light unto the World

Just as treasures are uncovered from the earth, so virtue appears
from good deeds, and wisdom appears from a pure and peaceful mind.
To walk safely through the maze of human life,
one needs the light of wisdom and the guidance of virtue.

~ Buddha

On February 20, 1976, the year of America's bicentennial, Gurudev became a United States citizen. That evening, at the *ashram*, he described the ceremony and expressed his appreciation.

> Thank you very much for making me one of you. But it really was only a matter of legality. Otherwise, I have been an American for the past ten years. Wherever I go, I feel that I am one of that group. The reason is that I really don't seem to belong to any one country.*

> In 1966, when I came here, they all called me a hippie, because I was in the midst of hippies. And I was happy to be called a hippie, since that is the only way we could establish a proper communication. Even when the nameless, formless God comes down to our level, that Supreme One has to take some name and form. Unless you are on the same level, you cannot communicate, you cannot even understand each other. For instance, if you're an adult who wants to play with children, you have to get down on all fours and crawl and talk their language. You may be a famous philosopher, someone with many letters after your name. But if you're going to use all your education with the children, they will get scared. They won't even come near you. So, you have to talk in their own language, crawl like them. Only then will there be proper communication.

---

*Gurudev held a world passport, of a kind that has been available for decades and that identifies one as a "world citizen."

So, as soon as I walked into this country, I felt that. And if you remember my talks, you remember that, very often, you heard me saying, "We Americans," because when you are in America, you are an American. . . .

To really know God is to renounce all your limitations. This is the reason why you see, in almost all the different religions—whatever be the country, caste or community—all the God-men and God-women have renounced their narrowness. No real sage or saint or prophet has ever said, "I belong only to this country or that group or this community and not others." It is we who limit them, because we are still limited by our own narrowness. When we are narrow, we say, "Moses belongs to us." "Jesus belongs to us." "Buddha belongs to us." We limit them. But ask Moses and Jesus and Buddha, "To whom do you belong?" They will certainly answer, "We belong to everyone."

That same year, 1976, marked the tenth anniversary of Gurudev's arrival in the United States. His devotees organized a grand celebration at the Cathedral of St. John the Divine. They were joined by 2,000 friends and students, including Sri T. N. Kaul, the Indian ambassador to the U.S., and interfaith colleagues like Rabbi Gelberman.

By that time, the pre-*sannyasis* had become *sannyasis*, full monastics, and they began to assume more responsibilities with regard to giving personal guidance to students.

It was around then that several Western monks recognized that the time had come for interreligious dialogue to become more formalized within the Christian monastic orders. Among them were Thomas Merton, the American Trappist monk and mystic; Father Bede Griffiths, the British Benedictine monk who served in South India and received special dispensation from his order to be known as Swami Dayananda and to wear the traditional Hindu swami attire; Brother David Steindl-Rast, the Austrian Benedictine monk who practiced Zen Buddhism and Yoga; Father Raimon Panikkar, a Spanish Roman Catholic priest and scholar specializing in comparative religion; and Father Basil Pennington, a Trappist monk and priest. It was through their foresight and their efforts that the North American Commission for Monastic Interreligious Dialogue (MID), originally called the North American Board for East-West Dialogue (NABEWD), was established, the following year.

Gurudev was invited to attend its first meeting, in 1977 in Petersham, Massachusetts (he was later appointed to NABEWD's advisory board). That meeting laid the groundwork for the intentional and organized involvement of American monastic men and women in interreligious dialogue. Abbot Armand Veilleux, a Cistercian, served as moderator, and Brother David, Father Mayeul de Dreuille (a Benedictine), Ram Dass, and Gurudev gave talks. In his talk, Brother David recounted his spiritual journey and his discovery of the relationship between the East and the West:

> At this point my contact with Eastern monks led me to a deeper understanding of the monastic calling we have in common, and at the same time I began to appreciate the important role monks are called to play in the encounter between East and West. The moment I came to know Buddhist and Hindu monks it became obvious to me that what we had in common was a methodical effort to deepen our awareness of that reality which gives meaning to life. We shared a radical dedication to search for the Source of Meaning and to drink from that source. This search and this drinking may be expressed and interpreted in a great variety of ways by the different religions. Yet, the experience as such lies deeper than all those interpretations. It lies at the basis of all religions and is their common root. Thus, I came to see monasticism as a basic human reality, and monastic vocation as a response more fundamental than one's allegiance to this or that religious group or creed. A monk is not a super-Buddhist or a super-Christian, but a person drawn to the monastic venture who happens to find himself in a Buddhist or Christian environment. Of course, that environment shapes and interprets the monastic experience, giving it a specific form of fulfillment. (www.gratefulness.org.)

He also described his meeting Gurudev for the first time: "We had something in common that was central to both of us: we were monks. That was a tremendous discovery."

During the meeting, Brother David drew on one of Gurudev's teaching metaphors, which led to a lively interchange between Gurudev and Ram Dass.

Brother David: Swamiji has said this many times. "Keep digging," he says. "When you're digging for water, keep digging where you are. If you dig long enough you will hit water." You may be just one foot from water, but you get frustrated and start another well. But it doesn't yield anything, you think, so you dig another well, and another, and another. I like this image of digging wells. If you dig long enough, you will eventually hit water. Wherever you are planted, bloom where you're planted. Whatever tradition you are in, follow that tradition. If you are a Christian you will find Zen, and you will find Hinduism. Nowadays, you can hardly bypass them; they will somehow come up.

Ram Dass: I disagree with what Swamiji said to you, David, about digging in the same place. I agree that, ultimately, you will end up digging in a place, deeper.

Swami Satchidananda: When you get tired of digging all over.

Ram Dass: But that tiredness must be gone through, that must happen, that must evolve. You don't bypass it because somebody says to dig in the same place. "You're only good if you dig in the same place," or something like that. It's not an order; it's an evolution. Now the reason that if you were a Westerner you would come into a Christian tradition is because it provides it all and provides it in the cultural context in which you grew up. That's why I came back to find Christianity and Judaism, and I did it through Hinduism.

Brother David: I see. So you are saying that, nowadays, there are many floating around and digging here and there, but they have to go through this process until they themselves want to keep digging in one place—not because they are told to do so.

Ram Dass: It has to come through the inner feeling of rightness of the individual. I'm not an institutional man. I don't represent any institution as far as I know. And what I keep experiencing is that it's got to feel right-on for me at the moment. I'm demanding that, and if it doesn't, I scream.

Swami Satchidananda: We are talking about different traditions, different institutions. They are nothing but mere labels. What do you mean by different institutions, different traditions, different religions? They are nothing but labels. You must, Ram Dass, dig the same well with different labels, that's all. You see, Ram Dass changed the labels, but he kept on digging the same well. He had one thing to know. He had one goal to realize, and he kept on working towards that. He used the Jewish tradition label for a while, another label for a while, now he's using the Hindu label for a while. Nevertheless, the Spirit is the same.

This tradition, that tradition, I really don't understand what you mean by tradition. In digging, as long as you satisfy your hunger, it doesn't matter what you eat. That is what I call "keep digging." It's not the labels.

Throughout the 1970s, Gurudev continued to travel extensively, giving talks all over the world. He also began to receive many invitations to address medical and other health-related groups. Indeed, at that time, the medical sector's interest in Yoga grew at an astonishing speed, and Gurudev's teachings inspired many healthcare professionals, including the cardiologist and author Dr. Dean Ornish, founder and director of the Preventive Medicine Institute, and Dr. Michael Lerner, cofounder of Commonweal (also a cofounder of the Commonweal Cancer Help Program), to create Yoga-based health programs.

At the same time, Gurudev's work on behalf of interfaith harmony also continued to grow. And, in 1977, he spoke more often about his dream of an interfaith temple, a permanent place that would embody the spirit of the many interfaith programs, retreats, and services that he conducted around the world. The temple would also be a sacred place where people of all faiths could come together under one roof to worship together silently, where the essential unity of all faiths could be experienced. Gurudev had held that vision for many years; it seemed that it was now time for the dream to be realized. Soon, plans were underway for the creation of the Light Of Truth Universal Shrine.

As Gurudev envisioned it, the building would be shaped like a lotus flower. The lotus flower is rooted in muddy water but is not tainted by it, and its magnificent blossom is always facing the light. In the East, the lotus symbolizes the spiritual evolution of the human being. Like the lotus flower that is always looking toward the sun, we will ultimately shift our awareness to the divine light within. The lotus also symbolizes the pure spirit that pervades the physical world but remains unsullied by it.

Inside the shrine, in the meditation sanctuary, a light would rise up from the central altar. Encircling the light would be altars dedicated to the various world religions, and from the center light, a beam of light would come down to shine on each altar, a visual representation of the Vedic teaching that there are many paths leading to one universal truth. Another way of expressing that is "Truth is one, paths are many." That axiom, in fact, became the motto for the LOTUS and for the entire Integral Yoga organization. In the LOTUS, people would be able to pray at the altar of their own faith while contemplating the unity that underlies the multiplicity of the world's religions and philosophies. The experience of spiritual unity, Gurudev taught, leads to global harmony, to cooperation, and to love and understanding. According to his teachings, understanding is the fundamental remedy to humanity's divisiveness, greed, and hatred.

With Gurudev's drawings in hand, artists and architects began to sketch their concepts for the design of the unique shrine.

In July of that same year, during Guru Poornima, the celebration of one's spiritual preceptor, Gurudev invited leaders of five major religions to the *ashram* in Connecticut for a moving ceremony that would convey the idea of spiritual unity. The five celebrants—Brother David, Rabbi Gelberman, the Venerable Gesshin Prabhasa Dharma (founder and president of the International Zen Institute of America), Murshida Taj Inayat (a leader of the Sufi Order and spiritual partner of Pir Vilayat Inayat Khan), Father Robert Beh (Catholic chaplain of the Washington State Penitentiary), and Gurudev—gathered around an altar to take part in an interfaith service that would honor the Divine in the form of light. Each celebrant performed rituals from his or her tradition while worshiping at the central light.

This innovative event, called All Faiths Day, reflected Gurudev's lifelong work in bringing together people from various traditions to worship together, helping to heal the religious conflicts that divided them. Five hundred people of all ages and from diverse backgrounds and traditions watched and participated in this powerful ceremony. There is a certain synergy generated during this ceremony that evokes profound feelings of empathy, love, and respect for all beings—in effect, a deep sense of unity. Moreover, these feelings emerge not only when one is representing one's own faith tradition but also when representing another one, and even when simply observing the service. Two guests who were there on that first All Faiths Day wrote eloquently about their experience:

> As we sat watching the pageant of All Faiths Day—the incredibly beautiful ceremony, the flowers, the candles, the hundreds of loving faces, the chanting, the unity of purpose—we realized vividly how powerful this day was and how important it was to the destiny of the world.

> We have been moved before in our lives. But the depth of our emotion that day distinctly revealed to us that if humankind were to survive, this would have to be the way, in a display of love and brotherhood and sisterhood that overcame all barriers, dissolved all differences, and demonstrated the great, overwhelming truth that we are all one. And in that oneness, we are one with God.

Sitting next to us was a Catholic monk from a nearby monastery. He wept openly—as did we—during the service. When Gurudev and the others in the circle of Hindu, Jewish, Buddhist, Catholic, and Sufi leaders embraced, we turned and embraced the monk. And we felt God's presence as never before.

~ from *Sri Swami Satchidananda*

The sentiments that this couple articulated so vividly were shared by many who felt inspired to support the creation of LOTUS, a permanent center that would embody and foster Gurudev's interfaith teachings, his mission, his service, and his vision.

Occasionally someone would question the need for a shrine that only Americans or those from abroad who were wealthy enough could visit. They wondered how the LOTUS could benefit those who lived far away. Besides, there were many other needs, at the *ashram* and everywhere else in the world. Was it really necessary to spend time, energy, and money to build another religious shrine? To these earnest questioners Gurudev did not hesitate to respond. He made clear that such projects helped to bring people together in order to recognize the same Self in others, which, he explained, was so significant that, in a way, it was "more important than feeding the hungry, clothing the naked, providing shelter." Why, you might wonder, would he make such a provocative statement? He elucidated:

What is the reason why there are millions of people starving? Is it because there is not enough food? Certainly not. The world has a population of about four and a half billion [as of 2014, it's more than seven billion]. We grow enough food to feed more than twelve billion. The world statistics clearly prove that there is plenty of food. Then why should there be hunger? It's because of the lack of concern about other people—the lack of love, of caring and sharing. It is the lack of these things that creates poverty and all the wars and calamities.

Anything that you do to realize the spiritual oneness will help solve all the other problems. Certainly, if we are aware of our spiritual oneness, we will not be fighting with one another, starving one another, stealing from one another. The very purpose of religion is to bring that feeling of oneness, not to deny people. Universal love is religion. If that were instilled in our hearts, we certainly would not give room for these problems.

Please don't misunderstand me. I am *not* saying that we should not give direct and immediate help to the hungry, the poor, the sick. On the contrary, we shouldn't even wait to be asked; we should look for ways to provide them with that help. What I am saying is that *we should not stop there*. If we stop with that, it is only temporary help.

The Hindus describe four types of charity. Charity in Sanskrit is *dhanam*. And the four *dhanams* are *annam*, food; *swarnam*, money; *vidya*, education, and *jnanam*, wisdom. *Annadhanam* means offering food. If I give you food, it lasts for a few hours. Afterward, you have to find someone to give you more food. If I give you money, *swarnadhanam*, maybe you will be able to buy food for a week or a month. Still, it's only temporary. If I give you an education, *vidyadhanam*, certainly you will be able to earn enough money, not only for yourself, but for your family as well. But, again, that will not guarantee your peace. Education may help you get money, but that won't make you a person of wisdom. There will still be trouble. Many people fight, not because they don't have enough food, but because they are greedy, hateful, jealous. So, even education is not enough.

But if you give wisdom, *jnanadhanam*, if you help someone to realize his or her Self and to see the same Self in everybody, then you have really given help in the right way. Once that realization happens, food will come, money will come, health will come, peace will come; everything will come. "Seek ye first the kingdom of God; everything else will be added unto you."

~ from *Sri Swami Satchidananda*

By this time, a Yogaville West had been established in Santa Barbara, California, and many thought that it would be the ideal spot at which to build the LOTUS. A few neighbors, however, objected; one man said that he didn't want to look out his window and see a "cigar-shaped building." Gurudev offered to plant trees or do whatever it took to accommodate the neighbor and hide his view of the LOTUS. The local environmental review board met to discuss the issue, and its members approved the project. But in the end, Gurudev decided not to build there. His reason? The LOTUS was not for him or for one group alone. It was meant to be for everyone. And if even one person objected to its being in the neighborhood, the adverse feelings would generate a negative effect. Thus, the search for a LOTUS site resumed.

Then, in 1978, Gurudev received two marvelous gifts. The first one was from the renowned singer-songwriter Carole (Karuna) King, a student, who offered Gurudev a 300-acre estate that she owned in western Connecticut. Gurudev was concerned that, in giving such a gift, Ms. King might be criticized by the press; also, he wanted to be sure that no matter what he did with the land—even if he sold it—she would be happy. She convinced him that she wanted to give him the property without qualification. The Integral Yoga members had many ideas about how to use the property, but none of those ideas came to fruition. Eventually, Gurudev sold the property, and soon the significance of the gift became clear.

The second gift offered to Gurudev in 1978 was another Connecticut property. That one was owned by the late Swami Tyagananda, who, at the time, was a householder whose home was always open to ashramites and Gurudev's guests. Located near the *ashram*, the hundred-acre property included a clear river that flowed over a waterfall; it was pristine and undeveloped, an ideal site for the LOTUS.

The work of clearing the land to prepare for construction of the shrine began in the spring of 1979. Gurudev had been traveling, and when he returned home it became clear that a change of plan was about to occur. He had heard that the winter months had been difficult at the *ashram*, and because of the cold New England weather, the heating costs were very high and likely to increase. With more and more people coming to the *ashram*, the food bills were also rising. The large organic garden provided a good harvest, but the growing season was quite short. Moreover, fifty-eight acres were not enough to accommodate all the families that wished to make the *ashram* their home. It was time to rethink the plan.

Gurudev had in mind a completely new plan, one that would include a search for different land in a more temperate climate. The new site would be large enough for a growing community and for a LOTUS. It would be warm enough for a longer growing season, so that food costs would be lower. At the same time, Gurudev made it clear that these were only ideas and suggestions that he was making for the ashramites to consider. He wasn't telling anyone that they would have to leave the *ashram* or that the *ashram* would have to relocate. He was simply asking them to think deeply about the future before laying the foundation for the LOTUS.

As might have been predicted, the prospect of uprooting and transplanting the community caused quite a stir, but all the members knew that Gurudev was thinking about their well-being and the well-being of others who would come to live at the *ashram*. After serious consideration, the entire *ashram* community decided enthusiastically to embark on a new adventure. They agreed to look for a new site during the winter, and if they were not able to find a suitable one by the spring, they would remain in Connecticut and begin building the LOTUS there.

Their solidarity served them well. The perfect site was found: 650 acres along the James River in Buckingham County, in the heart of Virginia's Thomas Jefferson country. The air was clear, the land was fertile, and the atmosphere was peaceful and conducive to contemplation. The magnificent property, surrounded by the foothills of the ancient Blue Ridge Mountains and overlooking the historic river, was purchased with the proceeds from the sale of Carole King's generous, heartfelt gift, the Music Mountain property.

At first, only a few people left for Virginia to begin the work of building a community. No one wanted to abandon, suddenly, everything that had been established in Connecticut. Even after a number of individuals and families had relocated to Virginia, the *ashram* in Pomfret served as a retreat center for a few years before being sold.

The emphasis was now definitely on developing the community in Virginia. In a ranch-style house on the property, people shared rooms or found space for working and sleeping in the attic; someone even created a sleeping space under a stairwell, while others camped out in tents. A pioneering spirit prevailed. Eventually, trailers were purchased to house people (including Gurudev) and provide office space.

In the spring of 1980, people arrived from all over the country for the LOTUS Lake groundbreaking. The valley near the James River was encircled by trees and the gentle foothills of the Blue Ridge Mountains. The air was fresh and vibrant, the environment serene. Gurudev climbed up onto a bulldozer and into the seat, started up the motor, and spent the next thirty minutes preparing the earth for the LOTUS Lake. Those who were following the bulldozer reported that at one point, as Gurudev was unloading a huge pile of earth out of the bucket, the very last thing to emerge was a bunch of flowers, which landed straight up on top of the pile as though it had been intentionally placed there. From atop the big machine, Gurudev said, "I am sure that by the grace of God and the good wishes of all of you, this great project of the LOTUS will be achieved very soon so the world may know that we are all one in spirit." What an auspicious beginning!

Of course, a project like the LOTUS required a good deal of money, yet Gurudev was not in favor of embarking on a large-scale fund-raising campaign. He felt that any money that came should be from those who deeply believed in the LOTUS and who gave joyfully. So, his students began planning ways to fund-raise without putting pressure on anyone. The Integral Yoga Institutes across the country organized fund-raising dinners and luncheons, and they held auctions. Children baked and sold cookies for the LOTUS. Architects and engineers volunteered their services in the planning and construction of the shrine, and students from all over the country offered their skills, talents, and energy. In these ways, more people were becoming aware of the unique shrine that would be dedicated to all faiths.

At last the construction of the LOTUS was under way. Gurudev directed all the planning and the organizing of the construction, often operating the big machines himself. He was so focused on the project that he spent day and night planning, drawing, and contemplating the design and fabrication of every aspect of the shrine. Gurudev was more than visionary; he was hands-on. As construction continued, the design took shape: the outside of the shrine would be covered with thousands of delicate pink Italian mosaic tiles; the building would sit majestically on the banks of a fifteen-acre lake. Gurudev designed the LOTUS so that it would embody the principles of sacred geometry, elevating the visitor from the mundane to the sublime.

According to Bhaskar Alan Deva, a Feng Shui and Vastu Shastra consultant (that is, one versed in the sacred science of construction, or architecture, in the Indian tradition) and Yoga teacher who was involved in the building of the LOTUS, its geometry is based on a number considered sacred in numerology: 108. The number one symbolizes the individual; the zero represents God; and the number eight expresses infinity. The exterior of the shrine is 108 feet wide. The inside of the shrine is fifty-four feet (half of 108) wide and measures twenty-seven feet (one quarter of 108) from floor to ceiling.

As to the mystical significance of the shape of the shrine, the lotus flower contains all five elements: it grows out of the mire, or the earth, into the water and air. The pink petals represent the fire element, and the space that these elements fill symbolizes the ether element. The geographical location of the LOTUS is also meaningful with respect to the five elements: earth (the foothills of the Blue Ridge Mountains), water (the James River and the LOTUS Lake), fire (the high summer temperatures and the *homas*, or fire ceremonies, conducted at the shrine), air (the fresh air of this rural region), and ether. The balance of these five elements creates a powerful healing energy. Moreover, during the foundation-laying ceremony for the LOTUS, water from the world's sacred rivers, earth from sacred sites, precious and semi-precious gems and crystals, and even a moon rock were buried in the very center of the shrine's foundation.

Visitors approach the shrine by walking through a grand archway incorporating symbols of the world's religions. They proceed alongside a long reflecting pool, leaving all worldly thoughts behind as they enter the building, silently, meditatively, through the lower entrance into the All Faiths Hall. There they encounter glass cases displaying sacred objects that represent the world faith traditions—Hinduism, Judaism, Shintoism, Taoism, Buddhism, Christianity, Islam, Sikhism, Native American religions, African religions, Jainism, Bahá'í, Polynesian faiths, and such secular "faiths" as philosophy, science, and the arts. In the center of the hall, the *One World* sculpture depicts adults and children celebrating global harmony. The sculpture sits atop a meditation chamber, under which the earth, water, minerals, and gems described above are buried. A *yantra* in the ceiling above overlooks the sculpture.

A *yantra* is a geometric form composed of visual patterns that represent the cosmos and various aspects of the Divine. These patterns or shapes appear in many cultures and are used in meditation to calm, balance, and focus the mind. When one prays or meditates in front of a *yantra*, one can feel the divine qualities of absolute peace and unconditional love.

Many years ago, a *yantra* revealed itself to Gurudev in meditation and it became known as the Integral Yoga Yantra. This *yantra* includes a dot in the center representing the first physical expression of the very core of the cosmos. The manifestations that emerge from that core are symbolized by the rings, petals, and colors within the *yantra* (see the color version on the front cover). The entire *yantra* is surrounded by an open border signifying that the divine expression is infinite and unlimited.

In the early 1980s, Gurudev added petals to the *yantra* for each of the twelve faiths that were to be represented on the altars in the upper sanctuary of the LOTUS, and he renamed it the All Faiths Yantra. This *yantra* reminds us that every faith tradition leads to the Divine.

114

The LOTUS contains seven *yantras*, one above another: the LOTUS itself, a three-dimensional *yantra*; the *yantra* embedded in the cement of the meditation chamber; a stained-glass *yantra* built into the ceiling, overlooking the One World sculpture; the center altar in the upper sanctuary that holds the central light; a star-shaped *yantra* in the ceiling of the upper sanctuary; the clerestory; and the cupola, with its golden spire.

In the upstairs sanctuary, the central column of light rises from the center of the three-dimensional *yantra*, its twelve rays descending on each of the twelve altars for the world's major faiths. There are also symbols representing these faiths, as well as all other known faiths and faiths as yet unknown.

It seemed that wherever Gurudev was invited, people asked him to speak about the LOTUS. Many began, in their own ways, to integrate the principles of interfaith harmony into their lives. And clergy from various faiths also began to incorporate Gurudev's ideas for interfaith services into their own programs. Gurudev could not have been more pleased. For his dream was that interfaith programs and interfaith centers promoting spiritual understanding and harmony would spring up all over the planet.

In the meantime, certain householder students had long wished to make a more public commitment to serve. Some were married, some had families, and some were single but felt that the monastic path was not for them. The idea of creating a non-monastic ministry took shape, and after many months of planning, the Integral Yoga Ministry came into being. That summer, during the annual Guru Poornima celebration, Gurudev ordained eighteen Integral Yoga ministers. Eventually, a formal seminarian program was established; at this writing, there are thirty-four ministers in the United States and abroad who are continuing Gurudev's service in promoting peace through the yogic teachings and interfaith harmony. They teach classes, give talks and workshops, provide spiritual counseling, and perform interfaith weddings, baby blessings, and funerals.

One could think that, at age 65-plus and with such projects as the new *ashram* community and the construction of the LOTUS to focus on, Gurudev might have slowed down somewhat, accepting fewer invitations, traveling less frequently. On the contrary: the invitations increased, and so did his travels.

In 1980, for instance, he gave lectures in California, Hong Kong, and Japan, where he was a guest speaker at the first World Zen Yoga Convention. He spoke in Montreal, Chicago (including at the seventh International Human Unity Conference), Vermont, New Jersey, Switzerland and England, and New York. The following year, in 1981, he spoke in New York, France, Belgium, Switzerland, India, Malaysia, Singapore, and Sri Lanka. He spoke at universities, Yoga conferences, interfaith programs and Unity in Diversity symposiums, in churches, synagogues, and theological seminaries, in hospitals and prisons, and in radio and television interviews. He met with well-known religious leaders like Billy Graham and the Dalai Lama and with American presidents—Republican president George H. W. Bush and Democratic presidents Jimmy Carter and Bill Clinton—as well as with the late prime minister of India, Indira Gandhi. Gurudev also traveled twice to Russia when it was still part of the Soviet Union, invited as a citizen-diplomat to share his message of interfaith understanding and universal peace.

In May 1984, while Gurudev was in Rome, he had the opportunity to have an audience with the pope, His Holiness John Paul II (now Saint John Paul II). It had been many years since Gurudev met with an earlier pope, Paul VI. Through those years, the Vatican had continued to be informed of Gurudev's interfaith activities. During his audience with Pope John Paul II, Gurudev presented the Holy Father with an album displaying an overview of his interfaith activities and the LOTUS project. When His Holiness inquired about his other work, Gurudev replied, "My main work has been focused on bringing the religions together. Mainly, I'm working in the interfaith field." To that the Holy Father responded, "That is very good. I am so glad to hear about this, and I give all of my blessings and benedictions to this work." Gurudev presented a LOTUS pin to the Holy Father, and His Holiness presented Gurudev with the Apostolic Medallion.

When Gurudev left St. Peter's Square, the huge crowds that had gathered to hear the pope speak were still milling about. As he passed through the square, hundreds of thousands of people cheered and saluted him. Some handed him flowers, others shook his hand, and still others asked for his blessing.

Gurudev's schedule continued at a dynamic pace. Almost nonstop, he accepted speaking and teaching invitations and met with other religious leaders worldwide. In 1980, he moved from Connecticut to the Virginia *ashram*. The *ashram* in Connecticut was sold in the mid-1980s, and Satchidananda Ashram–Yogaville, in Buckingham, Virginia, became Integral Yoga's international headquarters. Gradually, devotees came to settle in Virginia, in and around the *ashram*. Together with other volunteers, they staffed retreats, teacher training programs, and weekend workshops. They engaged in various types of Karma Yoga (selfless service)—welcoming and assisting guests, helping with office work, cooking in the kitchen, serving in housekeeping and landscaping, developing an organic farm, and participating in the construction of the LOTUS.

In 1986, the International Year of Peace, the LOTUS opened its doors.

The dedication, on July 20, 1986, of this singular monument signaled an advance in the movement toward greater spiritual understanding and universal harmony. At the height of the festivities, some 3,000 devotees, friends, and guests gathered at Satchidananda Ashram. As described in the first chapter of this book, it was a marvelous occasion.

The grand opening and dedication ceremonies had actually begun the previous day, with religious leaders and dignitaries from around the world joining Gurudev for the World Faiths Symposium held in nearby Charlottesville, the town often referred to as "the home of Thomas Jefferson." More than 1,500 people attended the morning program, where thirty-two speakers spoke on the theme "Truth Is One, Paths Are Many." One of the celebrants, Sant Keshavadas, poetically expressed his perception of the morning festivities: "The flower garland represents the unity of world religions. The group of speakers sitting here is a flower garland to God."

In the afternoon, guests enjoyed programs of sacred music and dance associated with the world's religions. As the date also marked the twentieth year of Gurudev's service in the West, at an evening gala devotees and friends paid tribute to him as a servant of humanity. During the program, Carole King introduced one of the songs that she'd planned to sing, "One Small Voice": "This song is about one small child who spoke up for what he believed in. And Gurudev is kind of like that child. He was one person with a dream, a vision. Then, more and more joined in; more will join…. It's a song about how every one of us can make a difference.... If it weren't for every one of us, there wouldn't be a LOTUS. But there is one!"

That evening, Gurudev spoke about God's guidance:

> I have heard many beautiful prayerful songs written by great saints. But one always stands out, continuously haunts my heart. The meaning of it is: "God, you are the indweller of all beings. You are omnipresent. You make things move; you make people move. So, who am I to do anything? How can I do anything? It's You. You feed me; I am getting fed. You

make me sleep; I sleep. You show me; I am seeing. You make
me happy; I am happy. You make me dance; I dance. And
not only me, but the entire universe. Therefore, I know that
without You I am nothing."

That prayer has become my guiding light. I never planned
anything. I never wanted anything. I'm not an ambitious
person. God has simply moved me from place to place. This
is all God's work, not mine.

~ from *LOTUS*

Afterward, Gurudev was taken by surprise when William Veprin, who
was then the national commissioner of appeal and of development
for the Anti-Defamation League, presented him with an ADL
award. Gurudev was named a trustee of the Society of Fellows of
the Anti-Defamation League of the B'nai Brith: "In recognition of
distinguished leadership and dedicated service in advancing the cause
of human rights, dignity, and equal opportunity, preserving freedom,
counteracting bigotry, and promoting brotherhood for all."

Since LOTUS opened its doors, in 1986, thousands of visitors have
come from all over the world to experience the peaceful, healing
vibration and the feeling of unity engendered when people sit together
in contemplation under one roof. The shrine is open during the day
for guests and for ashramites, as well as on Friday evenings, and all are
welcome to sit in silent meditation with community members at noon.
The only rituals held in the LOTUS are the interfaith worship service
performed annually during Guru Poornima, the celebration honoring
one's spiritual preceptor, and the monthly full-moon chants for
world peace.

Gurudev's vision of a temple dedicated to all faiths and to all paths,
religious and secular, had finally become a physical reality. But like
his love and his service, Gurudev's insight was far-ranging, and he
foresaw lotus temples springing up in other parts of the world. Within
five months, in December, members of the Bahá'í faith inaugurated

their own lotus-shaped temple, the Bahá'í House of Worship, in New Delhi, India.

Both the LOTUS and the Bahá'í House of Worship were inspired by the symbol of the lotus flower and they share certain principles, such as the oneness of God and of humanity. The Bahá'í House of Worship, however, expresses that faith's belief in "a world religion whose purpose is to unite all races and peoples in one universal Cause and one common Faith." Its website further states:

> Since its inauguration to public worship and visits in December 1986, the Bahá'í House of Worship in New Delhi, India, has drawn to its portals more than 70 million visitors, making it one of the most visited edifices in the world. On an average, 8,000 to 10,000 people visit the Bahá'í House of Worship each day. These visitors have admired its universal design in the form of a lotus and have been fascinated by the teachings of the Bahá'í Faith, especially its tenets of the Oneness of God, the Oneness of Religions, and the Oneness of Mankind.

The LOTUS, on the other hand, does not promote a one-world religion; rather, it's a place where people of various faiths can come together to experience their spiritual unity.

The synchronicity of the events—the inaugurations just a few months apart of two lotus temples—attests to the power and mystery of the human imagination. Furthermore, a second Light Of Truth Universal Shrine has recently been constructed in Tamil Nadu, South India. The new LOTUS is located in the village of Chettipalayam, at Satchidananda Alayam, Gurudev's birthplace, the family home now preserved as a meditation site and place of pilgrimage. The shrine was built under the direction of Sri K. Ramaswamy, chairman of Roots Group of Companies, trustee of Satchidananda Jothi Nikethan (a residential school), and director of the Integral Yoga Institute of Coimbatore. The inauguration and grand celebration of the new LOTUS took place on December 22, 2014, Gurudev's 100th birth anniversary.

Another project that Gurudev had in mind was the creation of a LOTUS University that would be located at Satchidananda Ashram–Yogaville, near the shrine. Even before the LOTUS was built, he described that project in an interview with Professor K. L. Seshagiri Rao.

Professor Rao, a Gandhian philosopher and a professor emeritus of religious studies at the University of Virginia, was interviewing Gurudev for *World Faiths Insight* magazine. Gurudev and Professor Rao had long enjoyed a collaborative relationship, and the two were discussing the concept of a LOTUS University.

Dr. Rao: It seems, then, that your dream is continuing in terms of some educational center or a university.

Gurudev: Yes, yes. But, again, even though the ideas and the dream come into my mind, I just leave it to the Higher Power. So I don't have any sort of big expectation or anxiety about it. The idea comes; if it comes, let it grow. Even LOTUS happened the same way. I didn't have a cent in the hand, but we started it, and it grew and grew and grew. Likewise, that also will happen with the university. I have that feeling, because anything that's good for the world will happen.

Dr. Rao: So, when and if it happens, the center will be in the form of a world religions university?

Gurudev: A world faiths university.

Dr. Rao: A world faiths university? But would that world faiths university be intellectual and theoretical like all the other universities?

Gurudev: No, no, no, it will be practical, also. People should come and live that life. For example, we may have a Buddhist clergyperson come. A clergy member of a particular faith will be invited to conduct a course, say, a three- or a six-month course. And the students should learn not only the theoretical aspects of the faith, but also the practical components. So, if a Buddhist monk wants to teach a portion on meditation, the monk and the students should sit and meditate. They should practice the religion; they should live that religion. It shouldn't be merely learning by theory.

As Gurudev envisioned it, the LOTUS University would offer programs in interfaith studies and enable students and scholars to live, study, practice, and conduct research in a peaceful, healthful environment. In fact, ample space for such a facility exists close to the LOTUS site, and the tranquility of the natural setting would make it conducive to both academic and spiritual studies. Perhaps the seed for such a project has already been planted and is gestating in the form of the LOTUS Center for All Faiths (LCAF).

LCAF staff members organize monthly interfaith lectures offered at Satchidananda Ashram-Yogaville both by Yogaville residents and by outside clergy and laypeople. LCAF, a member of the North American Interfaith Network (NAIN) and the Interfaith Cooperation Circle of Central Virginia, also organizes interfaith services. In fact, Yogaville staff members regularly conduct interfaith services during Yoga teacher training and various other programs. Staff members also attend and participate in interfaith programs offered by other groups, and they network with other interfaith organizations.

When we consider the impact that Gurudev and his teachings have made and continue to make on the growing interfaith movement and on the effort toward world peace, we may remember how, when people would praise him for his work or his accomplishments, he would insist that he wasn't doing anything. He felt that he was merely an instrument in the hands of the Divine. How else, he would muse, could he, an ordinary person together with just a small group of people with limited skills and even more limited funds manage to succeed in building and maintaining a thriving community, a Yoga village that welcomes residents and guests from everywhere and from all walks of life? And how could ordinary people like that manage to create the LOTUS, a major accomplishment and a unique expression of the unifying principle that underlies the various approaches, spiritual and secular, to the truth?

Not many would agree with Gurudev that he was an "ordinary" person. But he included himself in that category not because he was acting excessively modest but because he knew that we all have the capacity to accomplish what he had accomplished and even more. Also, he had transcended the attachment to the body and mind. He no longer identified with the "I-me-mine" paradigm, the ego, or the mode of illusionary thinking that compels us to think of ourselves as separate from everyone and everything. He had experienced the realization that his true Self was not the ego consciousness but the Cosmic Consciousness, that his (and everyone else's) true nature was *sat-chid-ananda*: absolute truth-knowledge-bliss. In that sense, he and we are all instruments of that Cosmic Consciousness. As Gurudev said, "The highest compliment you can ever pay me is to enjoy all the happiness and joy that I experience."

A sampling of the many messages received on the LOTUS Dedication, July 20, 1986:

In today's divided world, any and all honest efforts to bring persons of various faiths together to explore more deeply the spiritual dimension of human life are to be encouraged and applauded. The concerns of our world are many, as are the needs of the human family today. People are not automatons or machines determined by the forces of biology or history, but responsible agents for building together a better, more humane, more godly world. People of all faiths who recognize this have much to discuss, much to share from their spiritual experience, and much common cause to make on behalf of humanity. I ask God to bless your efforts here today in that direction.

~ Cardinal Francis Arinze, Pontifical Council for Interreligious Dialogue, The Vatican

It is my pleasure to send greetings on the occasion of the Grand Dedication of the Light Of Truth Universal Shrine (LOTUS). I share your commitment to the cause of world peace and unity among all people. You have my best wishes for a successful dedication ceremony.

~ Gerald L. Baliles, Governor
Commonwealth of Virginia, 1986

I trust this occasion will bring a new dimension in the interfaith and intercultural dialogue which is most needed in the present world.

~ Doboom Tulku, Director,
Tibet House, India

To a world torn by conflicts and confrontations, may the Light Of Truth Universal Shrine be a beacon light to humanity showing the path of unity, harmony, and peace.

~ C. Subramaniam, Former
Finance Minister of India

The LOTUS will be a reminder for all to see that as God is One, so are we all—Jews, Christians, Muslims, Hindus, and all religions—One.

~ Rabbi Joseph H. Gelberman, New York

On the auspicious occasion of the dedication of the Light Of Truth Universal Shrine, let us dedicate ourselves to the purpose of the Shrine—interreligious understanding and world peace.

~ Dr. K. L. Seshagiri Rao, Professor Emeritus
of Religious Studies, University of Virginia

CHAPTER 13

The Entire World Is My Family

The first day or so, we all pointed to our countries.
The third or fourth day, we were pointing to our continents.
By the fifth day, we were aware of only one Earth.

~ Discovery 5 Space Mission

In April 1985, a year before LOTUS opened its doors, Gurudev celebrated the first Light Of Truth Universal Service held in Paris, France. On this occasion, he was joined by Rabbi Shlomo Carlebach, four Vietnamese Buddhist monks, two Brahma Kumari* members, a Muslim cleric, and a Catholic priest. During the same trip, which took him through Europe and Asia, Gurudev journeyed to the then Soviet Union as a delegate on a peace mission sponsored by the Projects for Planetary Peace, a nonprofit educational organization dedicated to exploring ways to peace. In Leningrad (now St. Petersburg) he visited the Russian Orthodox Seminary and attended a service in the Russian Orthodox Church, gave a program at the Leningrad Peace and Friendship Society, presented the Ascension Day sermon at the Moscow Baptist Church, and met informally with a Russian economist, a television commentator, and a well-known actor.

A memorable anecdote from the U.S.S.R. trip describes a conversation that Gurudev had with the interpreter assigned to him. One day, after spending some time traveling with and translating for him, the young woman, who was a loyal member of the ruling Communist Party, finally lost her composure. She was piqued. Why? She could no longer tolerate Gurudev's frequent allusions to "God."

---

* The Brahma Kumaris World Spiritual Organization teaches a practical meditation method that helps individuals understand their inner strengths and values. On a global level, the Brahma Kumaris is a non-governmental organization in general consultative status with the United Nations. It has actively participated in several international projects to which Gurudev was invited to serve as an advisor; among those projects were the *Million Minutes of Peace Appeal* (1986), *Global Cooperation for a Better World* (1988), and *Sharing Values for a Better World* (1989).

So, that day, she challenged him: "You know, you keep mentioning God; but here, in the Soviet Union, we don't believe in God. We are non-believers!"

Calmly, Gurudev replied, "Hmm. You don't believe in God. I see. But do you believe in comradeship?"

"Yes, of course," she answered.

"Oh," Gurudev continued, "and what about love? Do you believe in love? And do you believe in peace?"

Again, the interpreter answered, "Yes, sure; I believe in love and peace."

"Well, then," Gurudev declared mischievously, "if you believe in comradeship and if you believe in love and if you believe in peace, then, my dear, *you are a believer.*"

The young woman looked intently at Gurudev. Then, a big smile broke out on her face, and she said, "Okay, I understand. Then, yes, I am a believer."

The story illuminates Gurudev's all-encompassing spiritual perspective, and, when questioned about the nature of God, Gurudev loved to relate the anecdote.

In October 1985, Gurudev participated in the International Press Conference for Religious Peace, sponsored by the Embrace Foundation and the Sufi Order and held at the United Nations chapel in New York City. The Embrace Foundation was a nonprofit educational foundation working to create better understanding among people of various religions and cultures. Gurudev was an honorary member of the foundation's advisory board and appeared on its television program *Great Visions.*

The International Press Conference for Religious Peace was, perhaps, the first conference where religious leaders from all traditions joined together to make a public statement declaring the need for solidarity in order for religious peace to be realized. During the conference, participants also addressed the need for objective reporting. More than sixteen religious leaders from around the world addressed these issues, and members of the media—television, radio, and print—attended. Among them were Pir Vilayat Khan, head of the Sufi Order in the West; Ajata Sharma, president of Embrace Foundation; Rabbi Joseph Gelberman, rabbi of the Tree of Life Synagogue; Mother Tessa Bielicki, a Carmelite nun; Sister Marie Goldstein, director of the Hope Center for Interfaith Dialogue between Christian, Jewish, and Islamic faiths (in Israel); Sheikh Mubaruh Ahmad of the Ahamadiyya movement of Islam (in Pakistan); the Venerable K. Piyatissa Thera of the Sri Lanka Buddhist Association; the Very Reverend James Parks Morton, dean of the Cathedral of St. John the Divine; and Muni Shree Chitrabhanu of the Jain Meditation Centre.

Sharing his thoughts on interfaith harmony, Gurudev emphasized that religion means spirituality; in other words, when we speak of religion, we are speaking about the spiritual level. "On the spiritual level, we are one, one in spirit. We are many in all other areas; there is variety, and there is unity. The entire creation is made for diversity. Physically, we're different. Mentally, we're different. No two minds can agree with each other 100 percent. As scientists tell us, two snowflakes are never exactly alike. We're made to be different." "Why?" asked Gurudev. "Because in difference there is fun, fun in life, joy in life. . . . Religion should emphasize the spiritual oneness, always. Let's not use the name 'religion' when we see the chaos. When the differences are emphasized, that's not real religion."

At the end of 1985, Peter Stewart of the Thanks-Giving Foundation invited Gurudev to take part in a program celebrating the twentieth anniversary of *Nostra Aetate*, the Second Vatican Council's declaration on the relation of the Roman Catholic church to non-Christian religions. Gurudev joined a panel that included His Eminence Cardinal Francis Arinze of the Vatican Secretariat for Non-Christians, Rabbi Jordan Ofseyer, a senior rabbi at a Dallas synagogue; Dr. Muzammil Siddiqi, head of an Islamic center in California; Rabbi Lawrence Jacofsky, director of the Union of American Hebrew

Congregations; and Dr. Fred Streng, professor of world religions at Southern Methodist University. The theme of the day was "Our Times: A World Celebration of Religious Friendliness."

Gurudev and Cardinal Arinze spent quite a bit of time conversing, and Gurudev shared with the cardinal discussions that he'd had with both Pope Paul VI and Pope John Paul II regarding the need for greater interreligious cooperation. The two clerics exchanged contact information, and Gurudev assured Cardinal Arinze that he'd try to visit him at the Vatican on his next trip to Italy. He did indeed visit the cardinal in Italy, and during that visit, Cardinal Arinze asked Gurudev for some suggestions on how the Vatican could contribute more to interfaith dialogue and cooperation. Gurudev offered the following: "I have one practical suggestion to begin with. I would humbly suggest that you consider renaming the secretariat; that is, that you consider replacing the term 'non-Christians' with a term more reflective of the interfaith spirit." Later on, Gurudev was informed that the Vatican had changed the name of the Secretariat for Non-Christians to the Pontifical Council for Interreligious Dialogue. Over the decades, Gurudev and Cardinal Arinze maintained a friendship, exchanging Christmas cards every year.

In 1986, Gurudev was appointed to the international advisory council for the World Peace Project. He also met with His Eminence Jean-Marie Cardinal Lustiger, the late Jewish-born archbishop of Paris, while Cardinal Lustiger was visiting Boston. In October, Gurudev returned to the U.S.S.R. and, as a special delegate to the International Conference of Religious Leaders, attended conferences in Leningrad and Moscow.

That particular trip was organized by the Center for Soviet-American Dialogue, an organization founded by Rama Jyoti Vernon, who also cofounded *Yoga Journal*. Including several of Gurudev's students, the group numbered seventy delegates. The intention was for the group of leaders from diverse fields to meet with their Soviet counterparts. For example, Gurudev and other clergy met with Russian Orthodox clergy, the actors Dennis Weaver, Mike Farrell, and Shelley Fabares met with prominent Soviet actors, and Dr. Patch Adams (whose life story was later portrayed in a film starring Robin Williams) and other health care professionals met with their counterparts at Soviet hospitals.

One morning, the clergy members of the group met with the director, the archpriests, and the professors of the Leningrad Theological Seminary and Academy. The question-and-answer session covered a wide range of topics, including peace and, more specifically, how they could ensure peace between the Soviet Union and the United States. According to the late Dr. Peter Purusha Hendrickson, a psychologist and an Integral Yoga teacher who was with the group, the seminarian representatives encouraged their American guests to work to change the stereotypes that Americans had of the Russian people. They reported that the Russian people's interest in religion was growing. And they expressed their opinion that the possibility of war would diminish if we stopped fearing and instead started loving one another. The discussion ended with interfaith prayers—and warm embraces.

During that visit to Russia, Gurudev and the group attended a moving service at the Moscow Baptist Church. Gurudev had been invited to give a sermon there the previous year; this time, the sermon was offered by an American evangelist. A member of the Peace Pilgrimage sang, "Let there be peace on Earth, and let it begin with me . . . ." Americans and Russians alike were so moved that they shed tears of joy as they experienced the essential unity between the peoples of both nations. The sentiment echoes a teaching of Swami Sivananda:

> A Christian thinks, "There will be peace if all people embrace Christianity." A Muslim thinks, "There will be peace if all people embrace Islam." This is an erroneous notion. Why do people in the world fight? Why do Catholics and Protestants fight? Why do Saivites [followers of Lord Siva] and Vaishnavites [followers of Lord Vishnu] fight? Why do brothers fight among themselves? The heart must change. Greed and selfishness must perish. Then alone will there be peace in the world. People merely talk of religion. They are not interested in practicing it, in living it. If Christians lived by the "Sermon on the Mount," if the Buddhists followed the

"Noble Eightfold Path," if the Muslims truly followed the teachings of the Prophet, and the Hindus shaped their life in accordance with the teachings of the Lord, of saints and sages, there would be peace everywhere.

Peace, to be lasting and constructive, must be achieved through God. There can be no peace without the Lord, or God. *God is Peace. Root yourself in Peace, or God.* Now you are fit to radiate peace.

~ from "Peace," *Integral Yoga Magazine*, Winter 1996

"Root yourself in Peace, or God." Easier said than done? It may seem so, but Gurudev offered a simple method: spend a few minutes, just a few minutes each day, in meditation. To him, those were the most important minutes of the day. And in a few minutes, we are not going to miss anything. As he put it, "The world that survived so far will survive for another few minutes without us. We have done enough damage or good, whatever it may be." During those few minutes in deep silence, without distractions, we'll be able to experience peace. Then, we'll be able to send out peaceful vibrations that will reverberate all over the planet. What's more, those peaceful vibrations can help calm millions of restless minds around the world; as Gurudev wrote in a pocket-size book called *Pathways to Peace*, the peaceful vibrations that we send out can even reach the minds of the warmongers in the world: "If they are ever a bit relaxed, forgetting their fretting and planning, your peace vibration that goes around will just sneak into their hearts. And that is enough; a little flick of the mind will change the entire polarity. Tomorrow, they may say, 'We don't want to fight anymore.'"

All wars begin in the human mind, and even a little peace can change the mind; it doesn't take that much time. During meditation we can observe and calm the mind. In other words, we can witness the qualities or the nature of the mind—its restlessness or, sometimes, its sluggishness. With such awareness and through deep concentration, those qualities become balanced, and when the mind is balanced, we naturally experience equanimity, or peace.

Yoga philosophy emphasizes that this balance, this equanimity, this peace, is the natural condition of the mind. What happens, though, is that our thoughts create disturbance. The mind in its natural state can be compared to a still lake. What happens when you throw something into the lake? The still water is disturbed; and, depending on the weight of the object thrown in, there might even be waves. Likewise, our thoughts make waves in the mind—and heavy, that is to say, negative thoughts make huge waves that roil the mind, thereby disturbing our peace.

In addition to meditation, all the Yoga practices, whether they work through the body like the Hatha Yoga poses or through the heart like Bhakti Yoga or through the intellect like Jnana Yoga, help to balance the mind and return it to its peaceful state. A simple yet powerful practice included in the *Yoga Sutras of Patanjali*, known as *pratipaksha bhavana*, is particularly effective.

Pratipaksha bhavana means replacing negative or disturbing thoughts with positive, calming thoughts, cultivating a pure, peaceful mind. Gurudev employed a vivid analogy to illustrate this process. When we need to replace the old grease in our car, we don't pull out the old grease. What an effort—and a mess—that would create! We simply use a tool to inject the new grease, and the new grease automatically pushes out the old grease. *Voilà!* The car is ready to do its job. Analogously, with a clean, calm, positive-thinking mind, we are fit to serve by spreading peace in the world.

Whether we're at work or in a temple or at home, we can be at peace. And whether we're aware of it or not, the peaceful vibrations emanating from us will benefit many people. When we're peaceful, in one way or another, we help the whole world find peace and joy. And about peace, Gurudev declared, "It's limitless. You need not have any doubt about this. We can do no greater service. It's important work. Let's do it."

During the next two decades, Gurudev certainly took the opportunity to spread his peace around the world. He traveled almost nonstop, accepting invitations to speak on Yoga, spirituality, holistic health, peace, and interfaith harmony. He attended interfaith and peace conferences, often as the keynote speaker.

Continuing on the path of citizen diplomacy, Gurudev was invited in 1988 to serve as the official chaplain for the Soviet-American Citizens' Summit in Washington, D.C.

The summit, co-organized by Rama Jyoti Vernon and Barbara Marx Hubbard of the Center for Soviet-American Dialogue, was made up of American and Soviet citizen-diplomats, including astronauts, cosmonauts, newspaper and magazine editors, film directors, trade experts, healers, and religious leaders. Robert Muller, former assistant secretary-general of the United Nations; Henry Borovik, head of the Soviet Peace Committee; Ted Turner of CNN and chairman of Turner Broadcasting System; Sergei Petrov, the Russian Orthodox metropolitan filaret of Odessa; Yuri Korzhenevich; rabbi of the Moscow Central Synagogue; Father Luis Dolan of the United Nations; Paul Temple, chairman of the Institute of Noetic Sciences; and Patricia Sun, psychologist and director of the Institute of Communication for Understanding, were among the more than 500 attendees.

During her introduction to the conference, Rama Jyoti described a citizen-diplomat as someone who acknowledges but does not judge the differences in the various cultures and traditions. Rather, he or she allows the heart to speak. She quoted Gurudev: "Let the heart speak. Love is the greatest force on Earth; it has no boundaries. You don't have to know a word of another person's language; simply open your heart. Let us all speak through the language of the heart."

The citizen-diplomats were divided into eighteen groups that addressed various aspects of human endeavor, for example, health, education, the performing arts, human rights, global security, and spirituality. Gurudev participated in the Religion, Atheism, and Spirituality task force and in the subgroup, Religious Interface, and he put forth the idea of holding an interfaith service, a universal peace celebration that would include all the participating religious leaders, as well as a representative of the "non-believers." His fellow participants enthusiastically accepted the idea.

As summit chaplain, Gurudev had the honor of offering the opening invocation to the entire assembly:

> Beloved friends, I am very well aware that we are here among some who believe and some who do not believe. Therefore, I would like to make this invocation as an affirmation, not as a prayer or to bring in God. Let us as individual consciousness link ourselves with the Cosmic Consciousness, which is the sum total of all the individual consciousnesses, so that we can gain enough strength to achieve what we are looking for in our lives.
>
> Let that Cosmic Consciousness that pervades everywhere, from a minute atom to the great cosmos, give us the strength and guidance to find the peace and joy within and then to share the same with one and all. As we all know, it is not only charity that begins at home, but also peace begins at home. Let it begin with us, and, then, let it pervade the entire world.
>
> Let there be auspiciousness unto all.
>
> Let there be peace unto all.
>
> Let there be fullness unto all.
>
> Let there be prosperity unto all.
>
> And may the entire cosmos be filled with peace and joy, love and light.

Gurudev also conveyed the following message during one of the task force meetings: "Peace is God. We have to find the one spirit, underlying all beings, in the various faiths. We are different in bodies and minds, but we are one in the spirit. Religion is just what you believe. It's not in buildings, books, or rituals."

During his own address to the delegates, Robert Muller talked about the importance of religion in relation to world peace:

> The religions have always had an instinctive feeling that we belong to the universe [and] that something very special is

happening on this planet. We must hope that the [leaders of] religions will come together, sit down, and give us again ten commandments of life.* The first commandment of *all* religions will be: thou shalt not kill, not even in the name of any nation or religion. We are fortunate to have here representatives of the religions—my good friend Swami Satchidananda and others—who know these things by instinct.

On a more esoteric note, at one of the other task force meetings, Ed Winchester, who was head of the Meditation Club at the Pentagon, brought in an "aura meter," a device that measures what Ed called a person's "peace shield," and he demonstrated its function.

He began by asking for a volunteer who didn't follow a regular schedule of such spiritual practices as meditation. Ed used the aura meter to measure that volunteer's peace shield, which began at a distance of about five feet from the volunteer's body. Then Ed asked to measure Gurudev's peace shield. He began measuring from the opposite side of the room, continuing to back up as the aura meter gyrated wildly, pointing backward away from Gurudev. As Ed stood in the doorway to the hall, he finally announced, "Swami Satchidananda's peace shield begins somewhere outside of this building!" Gurudev just laughed and shook his head.

On the final morning of the conference, everyone gathered for the universal peace celebration organized by Gurudev's students. Eight American and Soviet representatives of the various faiths, as well as of atheism, took part in the service. Among the celebrants were Gurudev, Father Dolan, Metropolitan Sergei Petrov, and Rama Jyoti Vernon. What a powerful moment it was when the celebrants at the altar, each holding a candle, lit the central light together as the entire delegation joined in by lighting hundreds of individual candles!

In November 1990, Gurudev was part of a delegation—formed by the Thanks-Giving Foundation—invited to the White House to witness

*Robert Muller actually composed the "Ten Commandments to Humanity," which he often read when he gave speeches.

President George H. W. Bush's signing of the 1990 Thanksgiving Day proclamation. The annual event commemorates President George Washington's creation of a national day of thanksgiving. During this interfaith event, Gurudev represented Hinduism; Juliet Hollister, founder of the Temple of Understanding, represented Christianity; Dr. Mohammed Abdul Raouf, chancellor of the Islamic College, represented Islam; and Rabbi Jordon Ofseyer of Dallas represented Judaism.

Gurudev was also one of the principal speakers at the 1993 Parliament of the World's Religions, the centennial celebration of the 1893 World's Parliament of Religions, that first formal gathering of representatives from the East and the West. Like the original parliament, this one was held in Chicago, with more than 6,000 people attending. Other major presenters included the Dalai Lama, Thich Nhat Hanh, the Very Reverend James Parks Morton, and Sri A. T. Ariyaratne, among others. Gurudev spoke on the theme "Spiritual Unity and Global Harmony."

Building on the citizen diplomacy in which he had participated, after returning from his visit to the Soviet Union, Gurudev was appointed advisor to the Center for Soviet-American Dialogue (later called the Center for International Dialogue). Six years later, the world was stunned by the sudden, unanticipated fall of the iron curtain and the demise of the Soviet Union.

In December of 1994, well-wishers celebrated Gurudev's 80th birthday in a grand event held at the Martin Luther King, Jr. Performing Arts Center in Charlottesville, Virginia. The celebration brought together friends, colleagues, and devotees from the spiritual, medical, and entertainment fields. The participants included the Very Reverend James Parks Morton, Roshi Prabhasa Dharma, Roshi Bernard Glassman, the late Swamini Turiyasangitananda (Alice Coltrane), Brother David Steindl-Rast, the spiritual teacher Dhyani Ywahoo, Professor A. Sachedina, the Pop artist Peter Max, Dr. Dean Ornish, and the actors Laura Dern, Diane Ladd, and Jeff Goldblum.

During the program, *Hinduism Today* awarded Gurudev the 1994 Hindu of the Year Award, one among several awards that recognized his notable service to humanity.

Earlier that year, the Temple of Understanding and the Interfaith Center of New York had selected Gurudev to be among the first recipients of a new interfaith award, the Juliet Hollister Award, at the United Nations. The two other recipients were Her Majesty Queen Noor of Jordan and Gurudev's dear friend and colleague the Very Reverend James Parks Morton. In 1996, Gurudev was invited to be an honorary chair of the second presentation of the awards, this time to H. H. the Dalai Lama, sitar virtuoso Pandit Ravi Shankar, and Mary Robinson of the United Nations Human Rights Commission.

In the following years, Gurudev received many other honors and invitations to meet with spiritual, political, and academic leaders. In 1998, for instance, President Clinton and the first lady, Hillary Rodham Clinton, invited Gurudev to Washington, D.C., to thank him for his spiritual support. In the same year, President John Casteen of the University of Virginia invited him to a luncheon at the university with Betty Williams, a Nobel Peace laureate and children's rights activist. Following the luncheon, Gurudev joined H. H. the Dalai Lama and Archbishop Desmond Tutu at the Nobel Peace laureates conference sponsored by the university.

After the conference, the Dalai Lama invited Gurudev to attend a plenary session in Washington, D.C., where a select group of religious leaders who had been active in interfaith dialogue would consider how they could work more closely toward furthering interreligious discourse and world peace. That group became known formally as the Interreligious Friendship Group, and in November 1999, it met for another planning session, hosted this time by the former U.S. president Jimmy Carter at the Carter Center in Atlanta, Georgia.

Also in 1999, officers of the Interfaith Center of New York and the Temple of Understanding invited Gurudev to offer an invocation during the interfaith service convened to celebrate their commitment to the work of the United Nations. That service marked the opening of the fifty-fourth session of the General Assembly. The secretary-general of the United Nations, H. E. Kofi Annan, his wife, Nane Annan, and the president of the General Assembly, H. E. Theo Ben-Gurirab, prime minister of Namibia, addressed the gathering. During the program, the Very Reverend James Parks Morton offered a tribute to Gurudev in honor of the fiftieth anniversary of Gurudev's *sannyas* ordination, citing his many years of leadership in the field of interfaith dialogue.

In April 2002, just two months before Gurudev's *mahasamadhi*, Sri Chinmoy presented him with the U Thant Peace Award on behalf of The Peace Meditation at the United Nations. Reverend Morton, by then founder and president of the Interfaith Center of New York, hosted the event at the center. The U Thant Peace Award is given to individuals and organizations who exemplify the ideals of the late United Nations secretary-general U Thant and who have implemented those ideals in the tireless pursuit of world peace. Among the recipients of this prestigious award are Pope John Paul II, Mother Teresa, Archbishop Desmond Tutu, and Nelson Mandela.

A fitting tribute to Gurudev and to all those noble human beings who dedicate their lives to serving humanity and fostering world peace!

CHAPTER 14

The Legacy

There will be no peace among the nations
without peace among the religions.
There will be no peace among the religions
without dialogue among the religions.

~ Dr. Hans Kung, professor of ecumenical theology
and president of the Foundation for a Global Ethic

Daniel Goleman, author of the international best-seller *Emotional Intelligence,* is also the author of another groundbreaking book, *Social Intelligence.* As its cover describes it, the book unveils "the revolutionary new science of human relationships." In it, Goleman maintains that "the most fundamental revelation of this new discipline is that we are wired to connect."

Wired to connect. According to Goleman, neuroscience has learned that our brain's design makes the brain sociable. That is, our brain is inescapably attracted "into an intimate brain-to-brain linkup whenever we engage with another person." In fact, states Goleman, "the most telling news here is that the social brain represents the only biological system in our bodies that continually attunes us to, and in turn becomes influenced by, the internal state of people we're with." In other words, neuroscience has discovered that *emotions are contagious*—literally. Other people's emotions, particularly strong emotions, activate the same emotions in the circuitry of our brain. Goleman explains that "when someone dumps their toxic feelings on us—explodes in anger or threats, shows disgust or contempt—they activate in us circuitry for those very same distressing emotions. . . . We 'catch' strong emotions much as we do a rhinovirus. . ."

Conversely, when we interact with someone whose feelings toward us are positive, we catch those emotions, too. What's more, writes Goleman, we are inveterate mimics, and our impulse to imitate is reflexive. So, when we interact with someone who is sad, we look sad; when we interact with someone who is angry, we scowl; and when we're with someone who is happy, we smile. Sometimes, these facial gestures are not obvious, but scientists who monitor facial muscles have clearly tracked what they refer to as "emotional mirroring." It's no wonder that the sages of India emphasized the importance of *sangha*, the spiritual community of like-minded seekers, where, ideally, members imbibe one another's peaceful spiritual vibrations. To quote the Vietnamese Buddhist master, Thich Nhat Hanh:

> If in our daily life we can smile, if we can be peaceful and happy, not only we, but everyone will profit from it. This is the most basic kind of peace work. . . . The Buddha, Shakyamuni, our teacher, predicted that the next Buddha would be Maitreya, the Buddha of love. . . . It is possible that the next Buddha will not take the form of an individual. The next Buddha may take the form of a community, a community practicing understanding and loving kindness, a community practicing mindful living. And the practice can be carried out as a group, as a city, as a nation.
>
> ~ "The Next Buddha May Be A Sangha,"
> *Inquiring Mind* journal, Spring 1994

One of the questions that arises out of Goleman's inquiry relates directly to the theme of this book, peace through interfaith harmony: What can help groups divided by hatred learn how to live together in peace?

Obviously, there is no simple answer to a question related to political, social, cultural, psychological, and, as we've seen, even neurological issues. Nevertheless, empirical evidence reveals that when people get to know each other through dialogue, formal and informal, when they talk together, eat together, work together, have fun together, pray together, and meditate together, something profound happens. Instead of seeing others as different and separate from us, our perspective shifts, and we become aware of our essential unity. In community, we experience communion. Our perspective broadens, our perception deepens, and our consciousness expands. We come to value the distinctions that color our lives as we celebrate the commonalities that unite us, one and all. Then trust replaces fear, and love replaces hatred.

Serving selflessly, meditating, studying scriptures and texts from various traditions, and working together to transform our negative thoughts into positive ones, we uplift one another. That is the purpose of community, of *sangha*, and that is the purpose of the LOTUS: they serve to remind us that, despite our diversity, we are one human family. They exist to teach us that, despite our differences, it is not only possible for us to live together in peace, but it is essential for our well-being and for our very survival.

Today many people refuse to affiliate with an organized religion, and the reasons for their reluctance vary. Some feel drawn to secular paths like philosophy and science. Others are reacting to the narrow-minded, hypocritical, and even criminal behavior shown by certain clerical authorities. And some people are spiritual minded but not religious in the traditional sense. As Robert C. Fuller puts it, these people "reject traditional organized religion as the sole—or even the most valuable—means of furthering their spiritual growth." Nowadays, in fact, a growing number of people refer to themselves as "spiritual but not religious" (SBNR).

Fuller taught physics at Columbia University and was one of the youngest people in the United States to have served, at age 33, as a college president (at Oberlin). He is also the cofounder of the Hunger Project, a citizen-diplomat who traveled to the Soviet Union in the 1970s and 80s, and the author of *Somebodies and Nobodies: Overcoming the Abuse of Rank* (2006), *Dignity for All: How to Create a World Without Rankism* (2008), *From Genome to Wenome: The Key to Universal Dignity* (2013), and several other books. According to Fuller and to some U.S. polls, including one conducted by the Pew Forum, 20 percent of Americans—that is, one out of every five—label themselves "spiritual but not religious." That number is up by 15 percent from just five years ago. Although the designation SBNR might mean different things to different people, it generally signifies that those who describe themselves as spiritual but not religious believe in some kind of higher power and have an interest in the "rituals, practices, and daily moral behaviors that foster a connection or relationship with that power" (beliefnet.com, November 4, 2013).

Philip Goldberg, an interfaith minister and author of *American Veda: How Indian Spirituality Changed the West*, maintains that the SBNR movement is here to stay. In an article on the *Huffington Post*'s religion blog ("Spiritual But Not Religious: Misunderstood and Here to Stay," February 13, 2013), he writes, "SBNRs who devote time to their spirituality are basically mystics—pragmatic, in-the-world mystics who probe the great mysteries from the inside out and try to live up to their spiritual standards." Goldberg draws on the findings of a 2009 Pew survey indicating that while many people leave their traditional religions, either changing affiliations or letting go of religious affiliations altogether, their spiritual experiences, defined as a "moment of sudden religious insight or awakening," reportedly occur more frequently now than they did in 1962, 1976, and 1994, when similar studies were conducted.

As Gurudev underscored time and again, though the names and the forms may differ, in essence "we are one in spirit." That doesn't mean that we should renounce our own approach. As he put it, "Real unity means accepting all approaches." That is what interfaith understanding means. It doesn't mean, as some assume, that all faiths must merge into one faith. According to Gurudev, that's not the purpose of the interfaith approach. In his view, "When things become uniform, they become boring. Variety is the spice of life."

The following excerpt taken from one of his talks delineates this point of view:

One in Spirit

In essence we are one. We are all related to each other. All we have to do is to understand that and to experience it. We are related in spirit. If we see the spirit in ourselves, we will realize we are all one. Your true nature is that of a spiritual and divine being. We are essentially spiritual beings made in the image of God. We are all the expressions of God. God multiplied into various forms and names. So, we can say we are the family of God; we are all sisters and brothers. We are all different colors, sizes, and shapes on the outside, but inside the same light shines. We may look different, but if we see the spirit, we realize, "I am you; you are me; we are one."

We should rise above all the differences and distinctions and see our spiritual oneness. We should learn to love each other, learn to love everyone equally. We should open our minds and hearts. Even just focusing on this one thought, "I belong to the whole world and the entire world is my family," will make one so happy and peaceful.

Living and working together as one beautiful family with total love is God. Real spiritual experience means moving around with a smiling, loving face. To see the spirit in others, and to love everyone. To rise above the differences of the lower nature and to bring harmony wherever you are. Ultimately, everyone should love you. Resolve that "I will live the kind of life that will make everybody love me, and I will love them." If that happens in your life, you will know that you are growing spiritually.

A real spiritual experience means to see the unity in diversity. See the same spirit in everything. Be gentle; be nice; be loving. See your own Self in all and treat everything properly. That is how to show the unity in diversity visibly and powerfully.

Know that we are all one in spirit; essentially, we are one appearing as many. The moment that kind of understanding comes, almost all other problems, both physical and material, will be solved. Anything that is done to bring this knowledge to people is the greatest deed. Any charity that is used for this purpose is the best form of charity. If we work toward real universal love and understanding we are going to the very root of other problems. Do what you can for this cause. Learn to care and share, to love and give, and inspire others by your example.

We need to use the spiritual teachings of our chosen faith to help us have real love for one another. It is religion that should help us to understand the spiritual oneness, to make us feel more at home as one family. If there is anyone who separates another individual, saying to that person, "You are different from me," using religion to make that claim, then he or she is not a religious person at all.

Thinking about these kinds of situations has made me pray, "God, use me in any way you want. I would like to see that in Your name, we become one family." If we want to be happy, we should work for the happiness of all people everywhere. That is the only way to achieve real peace and contentment.

In order to have a better world, we must learn to think of the globe as a whole. Your neighbor is God in a visible form. Let us have communion with our own neighbors—next door and around the globe. Let us feel that the whole world is our home and that everyone is our brother and sister. It's time to know each other and to live as one global family. To make the world right, each individual should find the ease and peace in his or her life. Once you have that peace, others will find many things for you to do to serve the world. Think that you are a nice instrument, ready to be used for the good of all.

Serve one and all. Then you will have served God. Don't even lose a single opportunity to serve others. Serve, serve, serve, and you will find that you also are served. Not everyone can go out and serve physically. Those who have that capacity should do so. Those without that capacity can project their positive thoughts. Those positive suggestions spread all over the globe. Those who have the capacity to do something physical as well should take that opportunity. Mental, physical, material—do something in whatever way you can. That is why all those faculties have been given to you. They are not given just for your own use. Your physical strength, your material wealth, everything is given to you to be used for others. Of course, that doesn't mean that you should not use it for yourself, too; but the major part of it is to be offered to others. That's the way we should mold our lives. You should not think that you are living here for your own sake. We are here for the sake of everyone. On every plane, we should be able to offer ourselves and our possessions for the benefit of humanity and the entire nature.

Prayerful thoughts always bring benefit to people. When ten thousand people feel for a person and pray, all that wishful thinking goes to help him or her. Good thoughts and feelings always reach the ones who are really starving for them. Those who deserve that good thinking will receive it. We simply spread the seeds. When people know that so many others are praying for them, that gives them strength. There is a benefit right away, "Oh, so many people are praying for me. All their good thinking is on my side."

My prayer is always that universal love will light our paths. Every day when you pray, repeat: "May auspiciousness, peace, fullness, prosperity, happiness be unto all. May all see good in everyone, may all be free from suffering. May the whole world be filled with peace and joy, love and light." When you say this, it's not just words; you really have to feel it, visualize it. It should be heartfelt when you send your energy out to the world. All prayers will bring benefit, so let us wholeheartedly pray for our world. Let us spend at least a few minutes each day in meditation. To me, those are the most important minutes. These peaceful vibrations will help millions of peace-less minds. Your peaceful vibrations, although you may not even realize their effect, will certainly help many people. You will be helping the whole world to find peace and joy. Let your actions help bring out that cosmic beauty and help to build a better world.

~ from *Integral Yoga Magazine*, Spring 2005

Given Gurudev's perspective, his philosophy, and his teachings, it's no wonder that providence led him to the United States, arguably the world's most pluralistic and spiritually dynamic society. In recent times, new groups of immigrants from the East have brought to the West new religious traditions that can seem strange to those who are not familiar with them. When first encountered, the rituals and customs of, say, Hinduism and Buddhism may seem quite mysterious to those brought up in the Abrahamic faiths. Thankfully, though—to paraphrase Bob Dylan's famous 1960s counterculture anthem, one that became a call for and an expression of social upheaval—the times they were (and are) a-changin'.

Nowadays, as we adapt, adjust, and accommodate ourselves to the rapid changes that characterize the fast-paced life of the early 21st century, we can take advantage of a variety of opportunities to familiarize ourselves with other faith traditions. Mosques and temples from the various Eastern traditions have sprung up in American and European cities and suburbs. Many private and public schools offer classes—sometimes required—in world religions. Numerous corporations now require employees to go through multicultural sensitivity training. Airports are redesigning their chapels to accommodate travelers of all faiths; some are even adding rooms for meditation and Yoga practice. The Internet provides listings of numerous international and national interfaith organizations (they can be found in every state in the United States and in many countries).

Additionally, interfaith conferences and both formal and informal meetings of spiritual leaders and laypeople from various traditions offer a way for us to get to know one another and to learn about other systems of belief. Television networks are broadcasting interfaith documentaries, panel discussions, and interview shows. The Interfaith Broadcasting Commission, for instance, whose website describes it as "a joint effort of Protestant, Catholic, Orthodox Christians, Jewish and Muslim groups," creates distinctive programming for ABC, CBS, and NBC affiliates. An outstanding PBS show that focuses on interfaith understanding is the acclaimed *Religion and Ethics NewsWeekly*, hosted by the veteran journalist Bob Abernethy. The program looks at the ethical dimensions behind the top news headlines. *Interfaith Voices* is National Public Radio's religion-news magazine.

Recently, the Richmond Forum sponsored a television panel discussion on the topic of whether Islam is a religion of violence or a religion of peace. The panelists were Ayaan Hirsi Ali, the women's rights activist, writer, atheist, and outspoken critic of Islam, who was brought up as a Muslim; Maajid Nawaz, executive director of the Quilliam Foundation, a counterterrorism think tank, and former member of an extremist Islamic revolutionary group; and Imam Faisal Abdul Rauf, an American Muslim cleric born in Kuwait whose aspiration is to improve relations between the Muslim world and the West. The debate was frank and informative, and the panelists conducted themselves with sensitivity and civility. This program was followed by an interview with a rabbi, a priest, and an imam, all based in Richmond, Virginia. All three clergymen have something very important in common: they love tasty food. So, they meet regularly and informally around a good meal. They obviously enjoy the food, but, most of all, they enjoy each other's company, and they learn, firsthand, quite a lot about one another's faith traditions. Their relationship is warm, and their appreciation of each other is palpable.

The paradigm of peace through interfaith harmony, crafted by peacemakers past and present, has established itself in the hearts and minds of those who recognize the wisdom inherent in an old adage, a cliché popular since the American Revolution: "United we stand. Divided we fall." In the spiritual context, Gurudev insisted that we need to do everything within our capacity to follow the principle that we should not—and must not—divide ourselves in the name of God and religion. What's more, we should educate others in the knowledge that our goal is to realize the unity and to enjoy the variety. Our objective: the realization that we're all heading toward the same ultimate truth while following different paths. His persistent entreaty that we replace our tendency toward divisiveness with the spirit of unity became particularly meaningful and took on even more significance with the destruction of the World Trade Center buildings in New York City on September 11, 2001.

Gurudev received messages from many people around the world, asking him to share his wisdom regarding that tragic event. One such request came from the organizers of a major Yoga conference held in Florida in November 2001. Gurudev sent the following message:

I am very happy to see that Yoga is more and more appreciated and embraced by people of all faiths and in all walks of life. Why is it so applicable to so many people and in so many fields? Because the essential purpose of Yoga is to keep the mind calm and clean. With a calm, clean mind we can serve well.

Now more than ever, we need to have a steady mind, a calm and clean mind, and a loving and compassionate heart. So many people are in pain, so many have lost loved ones, and so many are overcome with fear. That is all true, and we have to feel compassion and loving kindness toward everyone.

At the same time, let us remember that adversities are blessings in disguise. If we look only at the adversities, we will be consumed with sorrow, fear, and despair. But that will not help during these times.

Rather, it is better to remember there is a purpose behind everything. God has given us a big wake-up call. As yogis, let us have a deeper understanding and broader perspective when viewing what is happening in our world. Let's not focus only on the negative side. That is what we see happening sometimes, and people become filled with fear and anxiety. A yogi, on the other hand, will look upon everything with equanimity and balance.

Certainly, this is a very challenging time, but, ultimately, it's all for good. Look at some of the benefits that we can see right now. The two diametrically opposed political parties in Washington have forgotten their *party* feelings and are coming together, praying together, doing positive things together. People of various faiths are coming together, holding hands, and praying together. In a way, this tragedy is bringing us together more.

We are slowly rising above our differences and becoming united.

This is a time for us to remember that so many people have died in the name of religion. Now more than ever, we must understand that the purpose of religion is not to separate us. True faiths don't preach hatred and killing, nor did any of the prophets. It is the people who interpret the scriptures in a particular way who create the divisions. Division comes if we put our ego into the teachings of these religions. Let us strive to be free of that kind of egoism.

I don't believe in all the doomsday predictions. I consider this a transitory period. We are witnessing a great change. I see a very bright future for humankind. The positive changes that we are seeing are the proof of what is to come. I really feel that we are going to see a better world. If you want to know why I feel this way, it is because I see more and more people wanting to know the truth, becoming interested in Yoga and spirituality, and leading more caring and compassionate lives.

The consciousness of people is changing. They want to know how to lead a better life. And that is what I want to tell all of you gathered here at this conference. Please, have hope in your heart and trust that we are building a better world.

I send you all my love and blessings, along with my prayers. My prayer is always that universal love will light our paths. Every day, when you pray or meditate, visualize the whole world filled with peace and joy, love and light. You will be helping the whole world to find peace and joy. And you can carry this peaceful feeling from meditation all through the day, all through the week, all through your life. Even in the midst of a busy life, you can retain this peace. With this outlook, the whole world becomes a heaven on earth.

God bless each and every one of you. *OM Shanti, Shanti, Shanti.*

Active as ever, Gurudev attended the Global Peace Conference, held in South India, as its keynote speaker just before his passing on August 19, 2002. He was almost 88 years old, and some devotees were concerned that such a trip would be too taxing physically. To them he responded that when he did pass, they should celebrate, because, as he put it, he could serve much more powerfully out of the body than in it.

In recognition and celebration of his outstanding contributions to the interfaith movement, the Interfaith Center of New York honored Gurudev—along with the Honorable Al Gore, Jr., forty-fifth vice-president of the United States and Nobel Peace Prize laureate; Peter L. Zimroth, director of the Center on Civil Justice at New York University Law School; and Gaetana Enders, a humanitarian— with the James Parks Morton Award at their gala dinner on June 5, 2014, six months before the 100th anniversary of Gurudev's birth. In recognition of Gurudev as an "interfaith visionary," the center's officials wrote in a letter:

> As he was one of Dean Morton's most beloved contemporaries, this event would be a wonderful opportunity to praise Swami Satchidananda in this special centenary year of his birth. Our gala commemorates his contribution to advancing interfaith understanding through his timeless teachings and practices of Integral Yoga, his creation of the sacred Light Of Truth Universal Shrine that "celebrates the unity behind the diversity of the world religions," and his conceptualization of the All Faiths Yantra, a representation of all faith traditions within the entire cosmos, and his many dialogues through the years with spiritual leaders of many religions.

With the rapid growth of the interfaith movement within the past decade, undoubtedly Gurudev's vision, his spirit, his energy, his teachings, and the example he set as an advocate for peace through interfaith understanding will continue to inspire us as we move forward on the path to peace and unity.

It is important to keep in mind, though, that great spiritual teachers like Gurudev have always emphasized that if we want peace in the world, we must become peaceful within ourselves. Like charity, peace also begins at home. The Cambodian Buddhist monk and Nobel Peace Prize nominee Maha Ghosananda declared:

A peaceful heart makes a peaceful person.

A peaceful person makes a peaceful family.

A peaceful family makes a peaceful community.

A peaceful community makes a peaceful nation.

A peaceful nation makes a peaceful world.

While interfaith history might appear to be the history of conferences and organizations, it is in fact, as the Reverend Dr. Marcus Braybrooke points out in "A Dream that is Contagious," the history of "an ever-increasing number of people of different faiths and from different countries across the world catching the dream of a fellowship of faiths of our shared humanity."

Swami Satchidananda's vision of spiritual unity, his teaching that "Truth is one, paths are many," and his own example of a life dedicated to unconditional love and service are all points of light that lead the way to interfaith harmony and world peace. He implored us:

So, let us not fight in the name of religion. The moment the understanding comes that essentially we are one appearing as many, all the other problems—physical and material—will be solved. Until then, they will never be solved, because the basic cause for all the world problems is the lack of understanding of this spiritual unity. Wherever you go say, "We look different, but we are all one in Spirit. Hello, brother, hello sister." Care and share, love and give. Apply it in your very own life.

Gurudev's formula for global peace—focusing on the essential unity that underlies the diversity of our various faith traditions—is uncomplicated and commonsensical. That's why so many people who yearn to be peaceful and to live in a peaceful world are adopting that formula. Scores of them are finding their way to

Satchidananda Ashram–Yogaville, to Integral Yoga centers, and to similar communities and organizations around the world to learn and to practice techniques that will help them develop the awareness that peace is everyone's birthright. Admittedly, the dream of global peace is still but a dream. However, as we grow closer and closer to each other owing to the inexorable advance of technology and social media, to the tireless efforts and service of the peacemakers, and to the increase in interfaith collaboration and cooperation, the vision is catching on, and one day peace may—rather, peace *will*—become widespread.

Live a good life. If there are gods and they are just,
then they will not care how devout you have been
but will welcome you based on the virtues you have lived by.
If there are gods, but unjust, then you should not want to worship them.
If there are no gods, then you will be gone
but will have lived a noble life
that will live on in the memories of your loved ones.

~ Marcus Aurelius, *Meditation*

APPENDIX 1

Interfaith Luminaries

Cardinal Frances Arinze
One of the principal advisors to H. H. Pope John Paul II during his papacy, Cardinal Arinze also served as president of the Pontifical Council for Interreligious Dialogue from 1985–2002. During these years, Cardinal Arinze and Swami Satchidananda met, participated in programs together, and exchanged yearly greetings.

Yogi Bhajan (Siri Singh Sahib)
Yogi Bhajan brought Kundalini Yoga to the West in 1968. He created the 3HO organization, along with a number of other non-profit organizations founded on the teachings of Kundalini Yoga. He was involved in many interfaith forums, raising awareness about Sikhism and encouraging interfaith dialogue among religious and political leaders. Swami Satchidananda often invited Yogi Bhajan to join in interfaith programs, and Yogi Bhajan was a great supporter of the LOTUS, serving on its advisory council. YogiBhajan.org

Rabbi Shlomo Carlebach
A rabbi, a religious teacher, and a composer, Reb Shlomo was known as "The Singing Rabbi." Although his roots lay in traditional Orthodox Judaism, he branched out to create his own approach, one that included song-filled synagogue services. In a career that spanned forty years, Reb Shlomo composed thousands of melodies and recorded more than twenty-five albums that continue to enjoy widespread popularity and appeal. Considered to be a pioneer of the *Baal teshuva* movement—the return of secular Jews to traditional Jewish observance—and using his special style of enlightened teachings, his songs, and his inspiring storytelling—he encouraged disenchanted Jewish youth to re-embrace their heritage. Swami Satchidananda and Reb Shlomo enjoyed a warm and loving relationship, participating together in many programs until Reb Shlomo's passing in 1994. CarlebachShul.org

Sri Chinmoy

A spiritual teacher who dedicated his life to the service of humanity, Sri Chinmoy, in 1970 and at the invitation of the U.N. Secretary-General U Thant, began conducting twice-weekly, non-denominational meditations for peace at the United Nations for staff, delegates, and affiliates. "Sri Chinmoy: The Peace Meditation at the United Nations" continues to host interfaith activities to promote world peace at the United Nations and to present its U Thant Peace Award (Swami Satchidananda was the 2002 recipient). SriChinmoy.org

His Holiness the 14th Dalai Lama

Tenzin Ghyatso, the 14th Dalai Lama, is a Buddhist monk and spiritual leader of Tibet. Long a proponent of interfaith cooperation, His Holiness and Swami Satchidananda shared many interfaith programs and platforms together. They first met in Dharamsala in the late 1960s. The Dalai Lama invited Swami Satchidananda to be a member of the Interreligious Friendship Group formed in the late 1990s. DalaiLama.com

Ram Dass

Ram Dass (Richard Alpert, Ph.D.) is one of America's most beloved spiritual teachers. *Be Here Now*, Ram Dass's monumentally influential and seminal work, first published in 1971, continues to be the instruction manual of choice for generations of spiritual seekers. Having pursued a panoramic array of spiritual methods and practices from potent ancient wisdom traditions, Ram Dass continues to uphold the *bodhisattva* ideal for others through his compassionate sharing of true knowledge and vision. He and Swami Satchidananda participated together in many interfaith and spiritual conferences over many years. RamDass.org

Roshi Gesshin Myoko Prabhasa Dharma

A German-born Zen Buddhist teacher, Roshi Prabhasa Dharma founded the International Zen Institute of America and Europe. In the 1970s, Roshi and Swami Satchidananda met at an interfaith program; from then onward, she was included in many of the interfaith programs and services hosted by Swami Satchidananda. The two enjoyed a long friendship until Roshi's passing in 1999. ZenInstitute.org

Shaykh Nooruddeen Durkee

A Muslim scholar, author, translator, and the *khalifah* for North America of the Shadhdhuli School for Tranquility of Being and the Illumination of Hearts, Green Mountain Branch. Prior to becoming a *khalifah*, he founded the Lama Foundation and became close friends with Ram Dass, producing his book *Be Here Now*. Also at that time, Shaykh Nooruddeen met Swami Satchidananda when both were participants in the same interfaith program. Upon his move to Charlottesville, Virginia, with its proximity to Satchidananda Ashram–Yogaville, Shaykh Nooruddeen became a frequent speaker there and participant in interfaith services with Swami Satchidananda. GreenMountainSchool.org

Sister Maureen Fiedler, Ph.D.

As host and creator of Interfaith Voices radio, Sr. Maureen first interviewed Swami Satchidananda in 2002. Since then, she has taken part in interfaith programs and services at Yogaville. Sr. Maureen, a Catholic nun, has been involved in interfaith activities for more than three decades as an active contributor to coalitions working for social justice, racial and gender equality, and peace. Interfaithradio.org

Rabbi Joseph Gelberman

One of Swami Satchidananda's closest interfaith colleagues, Rabbi Gelberman, together with Swami Satchidananda, cofounded the Center for Spiritual Studies and the first interfaith seminary. A passionate pioneer and teacher of the interfaith approach to Spirit and worship until his passing at age 98 (in 2010), he was also rabbi of the Little Synagogue, president of The New Synagogue in New York City, a psychotherapist, and teacher of Kabbalah and Yoga. AllFaithsSeminary.org

Reverend Cannon Charles P. Gibbs

For seventeen years, Rev. Gibbs served as executive director of United Religions Initiative (URI), the world's largest grassroots interfaith organization, retiring in 2013. During the early years of URI, he and Right Rev. William E. Swing (URI founder and president) invited Swami Satchidananda to serve on its advisory board. Through the years, they enjoyed a warm association. URI.org

Roshi Bernard Glassman

A close interfaith colleague, Zen Master Bernie Glassman participated with Swami Satchidananda, for several decades, in numerous interfaith programs. Roshi Bernie is a world-renowned pioneer in the American Zen Movement, a spiritual leader, and an author. He founded the Peacemaker Community, an international interfaith network that promotes the integration of spiritual practice and social action. Roshi Bernie also serves on the advisory council of the LOTUS Center for All Faiths. ZenPeacemakers.org

Father Bede Griffiths
(Swami Dayananda)

A British-born Benedictine monk, Father Bede Griffiths journeyed to India in 1968. There he became a noted yogi, and he lived in India until his passing in 1993. A leading thinker in the advancement of Christian-Hindu dialogue, Fr. Bede looked for the universal truth at the heart of all religions. His *ashram* at Shantivanam in Tamil Nadu, southern India, became a center of prayer and meditation for many thousands of people. Fr. Bede wrote the inspiring foreword for *The Living Gita* by Swami Satchidananda. BedeGriffiths.com

Dr. Hari N. Harilela, GBM, GBS, OBE, JP

Chairman (now retired) of the Harilela Group, Dr. Harilela was born into a poor family in Pakistan. He emigrated to Hong Kong with his five brothers and two sisters. The history of the Harilela family is a rags-to-riches story. Leading business moguls and philanthropists who share a deep faith and commitment to religious harmony, they took Swami Satchidananda as their Guru and generously helped fund the LOTUS construction. Ms. Nalanie Chellaram, daughter of George N. Harilela (and Dr. Hari's niece), is the founder of Service in Satchidananda, an interfaith charitable organization. SISProject.org

Mrs. Juliet Hollister (Judith)

A great interfaith visionary, Juliet Hollister established one of the earliest interfaith organizations in America when, in 1960, she founded the Temple of Understanding (ToU). Among the organization's founding friends were Eleanor Roosevelt and Anwar Sadat. Mrs. Roosevelt referred to the ToU as a "spiritual United Nations." And, in 1975, the ToU's Spiritual Summit V was held at the UN—the first interfaith conference ever to be held there. Mrs. Hollister invited Swami Satchidananda to attend that Summit, and the two, along with ToU executive director Alison Van Dyk and Sr. Joan Kirby, representative to the United Nations, continued to be close interfaith collaborators until Mrs. Hollister's passing in 2000. Sri Swamiji's association with ToU continued until his passing in 2002. TempleofUnderstanding.org

Padma Sri D. R. Kaarthikeyan

Former director of India's Central Bureau of Investigation and later of its National Human Rights Commission, Sri Kaarthikeyan continues to devote his life to public service. President of *Life Positive* magazine, he receives invitations from all over the world to speak about human rights issues. He often organized programs for Swami Satchidananda, and he remains a great supporter of Sri Swamiji's interfaith vision. He also serves as a trustee of Satchidananda Jothi Nikethan, the school in India founded by Sri Swamiji.

Father Thomas Keating

A Trappist monk and priest, Fr. Keating is one of the principal architects and teachers of the Christian contemplative prayer movement. During Fr. Keating's term as abbot at St. Joseph's Abbey and in response to the reforms of Vatican II, he invited teachers from the East to the monastery. This exposure to Eastern spiritual traditions inspired Fr. Keating and several of the monks at St. Joseph's to develop the modern form of Christian contemplative prayer known as Centering Prayer. Since the reforms of Vatican II, Fr. Keating has been a core participant in and supporter of interreligious dialogue. He helped found the Snowmass Interreligious Conference, which had its first meeting in the fall of 1983 and which continues to meet each spring. He is also a past president of both the Temple of Understanding and the Monastic Interreligious Dialogue. Fr. Keating and Swami Satchidananda served together as advisors to the Temple of Understanding and during interfaith conferences. ContemplativeOutreach.org

Sant Keshavadas

Founder of the Temple of Cosmic Religion, Santji belonged to the ancient line of singing saints in the Indian tradition of Bhakti Yoga, or devotional mysticism. He established numerous temples and meditation centers and conducted more than thirty peace pilgrimages around the world. His motto was: "Truth is One. Many are the Names." His wife, Rama Mata has continued his mission since his passing in 1997. Santji and Guru Ma shared a long and loving spiritual friendship with Swami Satchidananda, and they often gave programs together at their many centers and over many decades. TempleofCosmicReligion.org

Pir Vilayat Inayat Khan

Spiritual successor to his father, Hazrat Inayat Khan, Pir Vilayat served as head of the Sufi Order International for fifty years. An internationally recognized spiritual teacher and master of meditation, he initiated dozens of international interreligious conferences and brought together spiritual and scientific leaders to engage in public dialogues. Pir Vilayat founded the Abode of the Message and Omega Institute, a flourishing learning center. He and Swami Satchidananda participated in many interfaith programs together, and he served as a LOTUS honorary advisory council member until his passing in 2004. His son and spiritual successor, Pir Zia, is a current member. SufiOrder.org

Acharya Muni Sushil Kumar

Founder of the International Mahavir Jain Mission, Acharya Muni Sushil Kumar brought to America a greater understanding of the Jain religion. In addition to Jain conferences, he convened numerous interreligious conferences and projects. Swami Satchidananda often invited Acharya Muni Sushil Kumar to speak at interfaith gatherings and at other occasions until Acharyaji's passing in 1994. AcharyaSushilMuni.org

Padma Bhushan Dr. N. Mahalingam

One of the most successful and respected industrialists of South India, Sri Mahalingam is chairman of the Sakti Group of Companies and a well-known philanthropist. He advocated fervently for the preservation of the ancient Dravidian culture and has ardently supported the creation of temples of light—light being a universal symbol of the Divine. Sri Mahalingam enjoyed a long and important association with Swami Satchidananda, hosting numerous talks and cultural exchange programs for Sri Swamiji and his students. He also took up the task of gathering soil, water, and artifacts from holy sites, which were subsequently set into the foundation of the LOTUS, and he generously arranged for the fabrication of the multi-faith altars and sculptures in and around the LOTUS. SakthiSugars.com

Sri Vethathiri Maharishi

A spiritual leader and founder, in 1958, of the World Community Service Center in South India, Sri Vethathiri Maharishi also established three hundred Yoga centers around the world and wrote over eighty books. Though he passed away in 2006, his legacy continues through the Aliyar Ashram, a residential center that he founded and the site of the Temple of Consciousness, which embodies the interfaith values that he promoted. He often invited Swami Satchidananda to Aliyar. It was at Aliyar that Sri Swamiji addressed the "World Peace Congress for Nonviolence and Harmony," the last program that he participated in prior to his *mahasamadhi*. Vethathiri.edu.in

Father George A. Maloney

As founder/director of the John XXIII Institute for Eastern Christian Studies at Fordham University, Father Maloney taught Oriental theology and spirituality on the master and doctoral levels. In 1965, he launched an ecumenical journal, *Diakonia*, designed to promote dialogue between Orthodox Christians and Roman Catholics. He also served as editor of all the Eastern articles for the New Catholic Encyclopedia. Until his passing in 2005, Fr. Maloney was recognized internationally as the director of Contemplative Ministries, Seal Beach, California. A renowned author, he wrote extensively on theology, true prayer, and Eastern Christian spirituality for Western Christians. During the 1970s, he often joined Swami Satchidananda at Integral Yoga interfaith retreats and services.

The Very Reverend James Parks Morton

Upon his retirement as an Episcopal priest and after having served as dean of the Cathedral of St. John the Divine for twenty-five years, in 1997, Rev. Morton founded the Interfaith Center of New York (ICNY). ICNY seeks to make New York City—and the rest of the world—a safe environment for religious diversity by fostering respect and mutual understanding among people of different faith, ethnic, and cultural traditions and by promoting cooperation among religious communities and civic organizations in order to solve common social problems. The James Parks Morton Interfaith Award is given annually to humanitarians working in the interfaith field. Swami Satchidananda received this award posthumously in 2014. His close friendship and collaboration with Rev. Morton spanned several decades. Interfaithcenter.org

Dr. Robert Muller

As assistant secretary-general of the United Nations for forty years, Dr. Muller devoted his life to the advancement of world peace. His ideas about world government, global peace, and spirituality led to the increased representation of diverse religions in the U.N. Dr. Muller was known by some as "the philosopher of the United Nations," and having created a "World Core Curriculum," he is recognized throughout the world as the "father of global education." In active "retirement," he served as the chancellor of the University for Peace, an institution created by the U.N. in demilitarized Costa Rica. Dr. Muller and Swami Satchidananda participated together in many interfaith programs, and, until his passing in 2010, Dr. Muller served on the advisory council of the LOTUS.

Padma Vibhushan Sri C. V. Narasimhan

Appointed to the United Nations in 1956 as executive secretary of the U.N. Economic Commission for Asia and the Far East, Sri Narasimhan served there in various capacities for twenty-two years. During that time, he arranged a meeting between then Secretary-General U Thant and Swami Satchidananda. In 1958, he was appointed under-secretary for Special Political Questions in the U.N., working directly under U.N. Secretary-General Dag Hammarskjold and with Nobel laureate Ralph Bunch. A close friend of Swami Satchidananda's, Sri Narasimhan often visited Sri Swamiji's *ashrams* and centers, and he served on the LOTUS advisory council until his passing in 2003.

Father Raimon Panikkar

A Roman Catholic priest who was the son of a Spanish Catholic mother and an Indian Hindu father, Fr. Panikkar became an early proponent of interreligious dialogue. After his first trip to India in 1954, where he studied Indian philosophy and religion, he noted, "I left Europe [for India] as a Christian, I discovered I was a Hindu and returned as a Buddhist without ever having ceased to be Christian." Fr. Panikkar lectured at Harvard and at the University of California; he wrote prolifically, and, in 1987, he moved to Barcelona, where he founded the Raimon Panikkar Vivarium Foundation, a center for intercultural studies. Fr. Panikkar and Swami Satchidananda became great friends, sharing a common South Indian heritage and a passion for interfaith dialogue. Until his passing in 2010, Fr. Panikkar was a member of the LOTUS advisory council. Raimon-Panikkar.org

Father Basil Pennington

A Trappist monk and priest who passed away in 2005, Fr. Pennington was a leading Catholic spiritual writer, speaker, teacher, and director. He also popularized the Centering Prayer movement that began at St. Joseph's Abbey during the 1970s. Fr. Pennington promoted a radical interfaith ecumenism, referring to Hindu swamis as "our wise friends from the East." He declared: "Indeed, those of us who are in ministry should make the necessary effort to acquaint ourselves with as many of these Eastern techniques as possible. . . . Many Christians who take their prayer life seriously have been greatly helped by Yoga, Zen, TM, and similar practices." Swami Satchidananda and Fr. Pennington participated in programs together, and Fr. Pennington graciously donated a Latin Hymnal to the Christianity display in the All Faiths Hall at the LOTUS.

Father Joachim Pillai

A Roman Catholic priest from the Kandy Seminary in Sri Lanka, Fr. Pillai became one of the first priests to engage in and support the interfaith services and programs that Swami Satchidananda organized in Sri Lanka during the 1950s. Their friendship continued long after Swami Satchidananda left Sri Lanka for America in 1966. Fr. Pillai came from Sri Lanka to attend the LOTUS dedication; eventually he settled in Canada, where he continues to serve his religious community.

Sri K. Ramaswamy

A close relative of Swami Satchidananda's, Sri Ramaswamy is one of South India's leading industrialists and philanthropists. As managing trustee of the Sri Swami Satchidananda Trust, he oversees its many charitable and social service activities. To name a few examples, the Trust has supplied running water to a village in need, it has sponsored medical camps, and it administrates the Integral Yoga Institute of Coimbatore and Satchidananda Jothi Nikethan, as well as many social service activities. In honor of the centennial of Swami Satchidananda, the Trust funded the construction of the first Light Of Truth Universal Shrine to be built in India, at Chettipalayam, Swami Satchidananda's birthplace. LOTUS.org and SJNSchool.com

Dr. Seshagiri Rao

Dr. Rao, Professor Emeritus of Religious Studies (University of Virginia), has devoted his life to the study of the Indic religions, Gandhism, and the ways in which Eastern and Western philosophies intersect. He has also dedicated himself to furthering interfaith dialogue at the global level. Dr. Rao served as a trustee of the World Congress of Faiths and as an editor of the *Interreligious Insight* journal. He was also the founding editor of the comprehensive twelve-volume *Encyclopedia of Hinduism*. While a professor at UVa, Dr. Rao met Swami Satchidananda, and the two formed a close collaboration that continued for well over twenty years. Dr. Rao continues to serve on the LOTUS Center for All Faiths advisory council.

Rabbi Zalman Schachter-Shalomi

Affectionately known as "Reb Zalman," Rabbi Schachter-Shalomi is Professor Emeritus of Psychology of Religion and Jewish Mysticism at Temple University and is World Wisdom Chair Emeritus at Naropa University, where he taught contemplative Judaism and ecumenical spirituality. He is well known as the father of the Jewish Renewal and Spiritual Eldering movements and for his pioneering work in interfaith dialogue, and he is considered to be one of the world's foremost authorities on Hasidism and Kabbalah. Reb Zalman shared the stage with Swami Satchidananda during numerous interfaith conferences throughout the years and was often his guest at interfaith programs held at Swami Satchidananda's centers. He continues to serve on the LOTUS Center for All Faiths advisory council. RZLP.org

Padma Vibhushan Dr. Karan Singh
A senior member of India's Indian National Congress and Upper House of Parliament, Dr. Singh was born heir-apparent to the last king of Kashmir and Jammu. In addition to his civic service, Dr. Singh has been chancellor of Banaras Hindu University and Jammu and Kashmir University, and he is currently the chancellor of Jawaharlal Nehru University. He has been involved in the interfaith movement for decades and serves as international chairman of the Temple of Understanding. Swami Satchidananda and Dr. Singh first met in 1989 during Dr. Singh's tenure as India's Ambassador to the United States. Through the years, they collaborated closely, speaking at many of the same events. Dr. Singh chose Yogaville as the site where his father's beloved Nataraja statue would be enshrined. Dr. Singh continues to serve on the LOTUS Center for All Faiths advisory council. KaranSingh.com

Brother David Steindl-Rast, O.S.B.
Together with Thomas Merton, Br. David helped to launch a renewal of religious life. From 1970 on, he became a leading figure in the "house of prayer" movement, which encouraged members of religious orders to deepen their contemplative practices and also introduced Eastern practices. For decades, Br. David divided his time between the life of a hermit and extensive travels on lecture tours. His writings have been translated into many languages, and his books, *Gratefulness, the Heart of Prayer* and *A Listening Heart*, have been reprinted and anthologized for more than two decades. Swami Satchidananda and Br. David first met in the late 1960s, and, for the next several decades, they closely collaborated on numerous interfaith endeavors. At present, Br. David serves worldwide through the Network for Grateful Living (Gratefulness.org), an interactive website visited daily by several thousand participants from more than 240 countries. He also continues to serve on the LOTUS Center for All Faiths advisory council.

Peter P. Stewart

As the visionary behind Thanks-Giving Square and the Thanks-Giving Foundation, Peter Stewart continues to nurture the organization that he founded with three other Dallas businessmen in 1964. Thanks-Giving Square is an oasis in downtown Dallas that promotes the spirit and unifying value of expressing gratitude. In 2000, a United Nations Assembly commemorative stamp featured an artistic rendition of the stained-glass ceiling that anchors the Thanks-Giving Square chapel. Swami Satchidananda and Peter Stewart began their interfaith collaboration in the 1970s, and, later, Swami Satchidananda was named a "Fellow of World Thanksgiving" by the Thanks-Giving Foundation. Thanksgiving.org

Sun Bear

Founder of the Bear Tribe Medicine Society, Sun Bear was a Native American spiritual leader who was, for a time, criticized by other Native Americans for sharing the practices and traditions of the Native ways with non-Native people. He had begun sharing this knowledge in the early 1970s, reporting later that he eventually gained support from Native people, and he continued until his passing in 1992. His message emphasized the unity of all humankind: "I pray that others may come to the path of unity that will allow us to overcome the enemy of separation that is now trying to destroy all the earth." Sun Bear participated in a number of interfaith programs with Swami Satchidananda and served as a member of the LOTUS Advisory Council.

Dada J. P. Vaswani

A humanitarian, philosopher, educator, writer, powerful orator, and non-sectarian spiritual leader, Dada Vaswani also serves as the spiritual head of The Sadhu Vaswani Mission. The Mission sponsors a wide range of educational and charitable projects, schools, hospitals, and organizations. Dada Vaswani is an ambassador of interfaith understanding and has addressed gatherings at the Parliament of the World's Religions, the Global Forum of Spiritual Leaders, and the United Nations Millennium World Peace Summit, among others. Swami Satchidananda and Dada Vaswani had a long and loving spiritual friendship, and they gave many talks and programs together in venues around the world. SadhuVaswani.org

Rama Jyoti Vernon

The founder and president of the Center for International Dialogue, Rama Jyoti organized programs that produced over 700 joint projects that helped catalyze policy changes between the U.S. and the U.S.S.R. She initiated dialogue programs for the former Soviet Republics of Armenia, Azerbijan, Georgia, and the Ukraine that led the way to the first successful conflict resolution roundtable between the warring factions of Armenia and Azerbaijan. Her successes in the U.S.S.R. led to invitations for CID to expand the work to the Middle East, Ethiopia, Central America, Africa, and U.S. inner cities. In addition, Rama Jyoti, one America's Yoga pioneers, cofounded *Yoga Journal* and Unity in Yoga, an organization that gave rise to the founding of the Yoga Alliance, the nonprofit association that represents Yoga teachers in America. Rama Jyoti considers Swami Satchidananda one of her mentors; she organized many programs for him and invited him to join several peace missions to the then Soviet Union. She continues to serve as a member of the LOTUS Advisory Council. RamaJyotiVernon.com

Wallace Black Elk

Wallace Black Elk, raised with his grandparents' strict Lakota traditions, was a Lakota elder and spiritual descendant of Nicholas Black Elk, the author of *Black Elk Speaks*. Present at the occupation of Wounded Knee, he was politically active in fighting for the rights of Native American people. He was a spiritual leader who served as an international lecturer and as a Native American representative to the United Nations. Grandfather Wallace spent a lifetime dedicated to earth healing. He participated with Swami Satchidananda in interfaith programs and represented, along with Grace Spotted Eagle, Native American spirituality during the LOTUS dedication.

Light Of Truth Universal Service Guidelines

The Light Of Truth Universal Service always focuses on light and emphasizes the theme of God as the Supreme Light in all the faiths. In the service, representatives of all the major faiths, and other known faiths, make offerings to a central light, following the order in which their symbols appear on the Integral Yoga® logo and the All Faiths Yantra®.

Organizing the Service

If the celebrants are traveling from afar, contact them well in advance to discuss the necessary items that they will either bring with them or that you will supply. If the celebrants are special guest invitees, it's helpful to assign someone to assist each guest with any special needs.

Meet with the celebrants the day before the service to discuss the manner and order of the service, the nature of their individual offerings, the time allotted to each celebrant, and any special needs they might have. Encourage celebrants to wear traditional garb.

The Worship Site

The worship site is set up so that the celebrants are facing the central light and directing their offerings to it. Members of the congregation are seated, so that they may comfortably observe the service. There should be an easy-access passageway to accommodate the celebrants during an opening processional, the distribution of *prasad* (sanctified food), and the closing recessional.

Three possible seating arrangements:

1. Have a round-shaped table to serve as an altar with the celebrants seated in a circle around the altar and the congregation seated in an outer circle surrounding them. The celebrants may then rise in place, facing the central light, and make their offerings.

2. Have a circular altar in the center of the room, with the celebrants seated in a semicircle or in rows in front of the altar and the congregation seated in semicircles or rows behind the celebrants. The celebrants can then rise, adjust their positions, if necessary, so that they are standing directly before the central light when they make their offerings.

3. Have a circular altar in the front of the room, with the celebrants seated to the side (either all on one side or half on one side and half on the other), with the congregation seated behind them. The celebrants can then rise and stand before the central light to make their offerings. Celebrants would stand to the side so as not to obstruct the congregation's view.

Articles to be used by the celebrants may be placed either on the altar itself or on small tables nearby, or they may be held by assistants.

The altar itself may be simply and beautifully arranged. The main article on it should be a large candle symbolizing the Supreme Light.

With respect to decorating the site, it is the most inspirational when the symbols for the various faiths, as they are depicted in the Integral Yoga logo and the All Faiths Yantra, are prominently displayed. You may hang banners for all the symbols around the room, or you might use a beautiful rendering of the logo.

Prelude

- Welcome and introduction by the emcee
- Invocation by a special guest

The Processional

Music may be played before and during the processional.

The celebrants enter in a slow, reverent manner, beginning with the representative of the youngest faith and proceeding to the oldest, as follows: Native American, African, Sikh, Islamic, Christian, Buddhist, Tao, Shinto, Jewish, and Hindu. Next comes the representative for other known faiths. Each celebrant carries a lit taper and proceeds until he or she is standing at the central light, facing the congregation. The processional music stops, and a gong may be rung as a signal for the celebrants to light the central candle together. The individual tapers are then extinguished, and the celebrants take their seats.

If a recessional is included at the end of the service, the celebrants would relight their candles from the central light and would then leave in an order opposite from that in which they entered.

The Service

The service is formed around offerings to and about the light, as represented by the central candle. Then, in order from the youngest to the oldest faith, each celebrant makes his or her offering.

Preceding the offering of each celebrant, a one-minute CD musical selection from each faith may be played. The two- to three-minute offerings may take the form of a traditional ritual practice and/or a prayer from the scriptures about God as light or a prayer on that theme composed by the celebrant. It is very inspiring when the offering is made in English, but it is even more inspiring when it's expressed in the original language and in the traditional manner. The emcee need only mention the faith represented. No historical or factual information about the faith is given, either by the emcee or by the celebrant. Also, it is not necessary to mention the scripture from which the prayer is taken. The last offering may be a minute of silence for other known faiths or a prayer offered in honor of other known faiths by a special guest.

Suggested format for the end of the service:

After the last offering, the emcee calls for "a sign of peace to be offered to one another by the celebrants and also by the congregation." Afterward a gong is rung as celebrants relight their candles and begin a recessional accompanied by appropriate music.

An interfaith message by one of the celebrants may be offered. The emcee may lead closing prayers.

Prasad

During the distribution of *prasad* (a blessed offering), music may be played. The *prasad* may be simple or more elaborate. Its nature should be determined according to the context in which the service is being held, the nature of the site, the size of the congregation, and the celebrants who are officiating. Please consider the comfort and convenience of all, and have ushers assigned to see that matters proceed as efficiently, easefully, and gracefully as possible.

Some suggestions for prasad:

- Each celebrant distributes a separate *prasad* item, reflecting his or her tradition. This can be in the form of food, drink, incense, flowers, the written word, or the like. The congregation comes up to receive *prasad*.

- The *prasad* may be distributed by assistants who receive it from the celebrants and then circulate through the congregation to distribute it.

Conclusion

The interfaith service is meant to be a reverent, joyous experience that uplifts, inspires, and fills everyone with a deep sense of their essential oneness. Rooted in the knowledge of that oneness, we can fully appreciate, respect, and enjoy the diversity that surrounds us, living in peace and harmony as one spiritual community in the light of truth. *OM Shanti* [OM peace].

APPENDIX 3

LOTUS Center for All Faiths (LCAF)

MISSION

The mission of the LOTUS Center for All Faiths (LCAF) is to promote world peace and interfaith harmony through a greater understanding of the unity underlying the diversity of the various spiritual paths.

PURPOSE

The outreach arm of the Light Of Truth Universal Shrine (LOTUS) at Satchidananda Ashram–Yogaville, LCAF organizes educational interfaith programs—including a year-long series of classes at Yogaville on each of the faiths depicted on the Integral Yoga Yantra—it oversees the celebration of the main holidays of the major faith traditions, and it coordinates interfaith prayer services at Yogaville. Additionally, LCAF staff members attend interfaith gatherings coordinated by other organizations and they invite representatives from local and national faith-based groups to give talks at Yogaville.

LOTUS Center for World Faiths (LCWF) was created in 1996 by Sri Swami Satchidananda. The name was changed to LOTUS Center for All Faiths in 2012 to include the many spiritual paths that exist in addition to the major world faiths.

GOALS

LCAF's long-term goals are to facilitate more interfaith programs and retreats, to create an interfaith resource center, to develop both printed and digital educational materials that will advance interfaith understanding, and to realize Swami Satchidananda's dream of a LOTUS University.

ACTIVITIES

In addition to its programs, LCAF has been involved in a variety of multimedia projects. These include:

- LOTUS.org: the Light Of Truth Universal Shrine website;

- *LOTUS: Light Of Truth Universal Shrine*: a full color book about the shrine and world faiths;

- Documentaries: *The Interfaith Vision of Sri Swami Satchidananda, Many Paths, One Truth, and With One Voice*;

- Interfaith Calendar: annual full color printed calendar that includes multi-faith holidays and observances.

COLLABORATIONS

LCAF actively collaborates with other interfaith organizations:

- LCAF is a member of the Cooperation Circle of Central Virginia (a part of the United Religions Initiative), the North American Interfaith Network (NAIN), and the Temple of Understanding, among other such organizations.

- LCAF continues its outreach work through staff members' attendance at such interfaith events as Interfaith Harmony Week at The United Nations in New York, the Islamic Society of North America's annual conventions in Washington D.C., NAIN annual conferences, Parliament of the World's Religions gatherings.

- LCAF staff members have served on the board of National Public Radio's *Interfaith Voices*.

- LCAF has an honorary advisory council of notable interfaith advocates who support the mission and vision of the LOTUS and LCAF.

CONTACT INFORMATION

LOTUS Center for All Faiths
1 LOTUS Plaza
Buckingham, Virginia 23921
Telephone: 434-969-3121, extension 110
Email: LotusCenterAllFaiths@gmail.com
Website: www.LOTUS.org

BIBLIOGRAPHY

Bering, Jesse. *The Belief Instinct: The Psychology of Souls, Destiny, and the Meaning of Life*. New York: W. W. Norton, 2012.

Bordow, Sita et al., eds. *Sri Swami Satchidananda*. Buckingham: Integral Yoga Publications, 1986.

Bruce, Ray and Goodsmith, Martin. *GURUS*. London: CTVC Production for Channel 4, (British Public Service Television). Documentary. Narrated by Sir Ben Kingsley, the documentary follows two monks from different traditions: Brother James Kimpton, originally from Wales, a monk in the Roman Catholic De La Salle order who served in the East, and Sri Swami Satchidananda, an Indian monk whose service led him to the West.

Flannery, Austin, O. P., ed. *Nostre Aetate*. Northport: Costello Publishing, 1996.

Fuller, Robert C. *Somebodies and Nobodies: Overcoming the Abuse of Rank*. Gabriola Island: New Society, 2004.

_____, *Dignity for All: How to Create a World, without Rankism*. San Francisco: Berrett-Koehler, 2008.

_____, *From Genome to Wenome: The Key to Universal Dignity*. Boston: Addison-Wesley, 1969.

Goldberg, Philip. *American Veda: How Indian Spirituality Changed the West*. New York: Harmony Books, 2010.

Goleman, Daniel. *Social Intelligence*. New York: Bantam Dell, 2006.

Hinnell, John R. *The Penguin Handbook of the World's Living Religions*. London: Penguin, 2010.

Hooper, Richard, ed. *The Essential Mystics, Poets, Saints, and Sages*. Charlottesville: Hampton Roads Publishing Company, Inc., 2013.

Karunananda, Swami, ed. *The LOTUS Prayer Book: A Prayer For Every Heart*. Buckingham: Integral Yoga Publications, 1986.

LOTUS: The Light of Truth Universal Shrine. Buckingham: Integral Yoga Publications, 2006.

Miller, William. *The Business of May Next: James Madison and the Founding*. Charlottesville: University of Virginia, 1993.

Norenzayan, Ara. *Big Gods: How Religion Transformed Cooperation and Conflict*. Princeton: Princeton University Press, 2013.

Satchidananda, Swami. *Adversity and Awakening*. Buckingham: Integral Yoga Publications, 2012.

_____. *Heaven on Earth*. Buckingham: Integral Yoga Publications, 2004.

_____. *Pathways to Peace*. Buckingham: Integral Yoga Publications, 2004.

_____, translation and commentary. *The Yoga Sutras of Patanjali*. Buckingham: Integral Yoga Publications, 2012.

_____. *To Know Your Self*. Buckingham: Integral Yoga Publications, 1978.

Sullivan, Sr. Maureen. *101 Questions and Answers on Vatican II*. Mahway: Paulist Press, 2002.

_____. *The Road to Vatican II: Key Changes in Theology*. Mahwah: Paulist Press, 2007.

Zaslow, Rabbi David. *Jesus: First Century Rabbi*. Brewster: Paraclete Press, 2014.

ABOUT SRI SWAMI SATCHIDANANDA

Sri Swami Satchidananda was one of the great Yoga masters to bring the classical Yoga tradition to the West in the 1960s. He taught Yoga postures and meditation, and he introduced students to a vegetarian diet and a more compassionate lifestyle.

During this period of cultural awakening, iconic Pop artist Peter Max and a small circle of his artist friends invited Sri Swamiji to extend an intended two-day visit to New York City so that they could learn from him the secret of attaining physical health, mental peace, and spiritual enlightenment.

Three years later, when he delivered the official opening remarks at the 1969 Woodstock Music and Art Festival, he led some half a million American youth in chanting *OM*, and he became known as "the Woodstock Guru."

The distinctive teachings that he brought with him integrate the physical discipline of Yoga, the spiritual philosophy of India, and the interfaith ideals that he pioneered. Those techniques and concepts influenced a generation and spawned a Yoga culture that is flourishing today. Currently, more than twenty million Americans practice Yoga as a means for managing stress, promoting health, slowing down the aging process, and creating a more meaningful life.

The teachings of Swami Satchidananda have entered the mainstream, and there are now thousands of Integral Yoga® teachers around the globe. Integral Yoga Institutes, teaching centers, and certified teachers throughout the United States and abroad offer classes, workshops, retreats, and teacher training programs featuring all aspects of Integral Yoga. Integral Yoga is the foundation of Dr. Dean Ornish's landmark work in reversing heart disease and Dr. Michael Lerner's noted Commonweal Cancer Help program.

In 1979, Sri Swamiji was inspired to establish Satchidananda Ashram–Yogaville. Founded on his teachings, it is a place where people of different faiths and backgrounds can come to realize their essential oneness. One of the focal points of Yogaville is the Light Of Truth Universal Shrine (LOTUS). This unique interfaith shrine honors the spirit that unites all the world religions while it celebrates their diversity. People from all over the world come there to meditate and pray.

Over the years, Sri Swamiji received many honors for his public service, including the Juliet Hollister Interfaith Award presented at the United Nations and, in 2002, the U Thant Peace Award. On the occasion of his birth centennial in 2014, he was posthumously honored with the James Parks Morton Interfaith Award by the Interfaith Center of New York.

In addition, he served on the advisory boards of many Yoga, world peace, and interfaith organizations. He is the author of numerous books on Yoga and is the subject of the documentary, *Living Yoga: The Life and Teachings of Swami Satchidananda*.

In 2002, Sri Swamiji entered *mahasamadhi* (a God-realized soul's conscious final exit from the body).

For more information, visit: www.swamisatchidananda.org and www.yogaville.org.

About the Author

Reverend Sandra Kumari de Sachy, Ed.D., has been practicing Integral Yoga since 1980. She became a certified Integral Yoga teacher in 1981 and was ordained as an Integral Yoga minister in 1995.

She has taught Hatha Yoga, Yoga philosophy, and meditation in colleges and universities, in Yoga centers and in prison, and she continues to teach and serve at Satchidananda Ashram-Yogaville. She is vice-chairperson of Satchidananda Ashram's Spiritual Life Board, a member of its board of trustees, and a staff member of the LOTUS Center For All Faiths (LCAF). She also teaches a weekly sacred text class to participants of the Ashram Yogi work/study program, focusing on texts from the various faith traditions.

Reverend Kumari has an M.A. in English literature and a doctorate in English education/language arts, and she has taught English in colleges and universities in the United States and in France. In addition to this book, she is the author of *Bound to be Free: The Liberating Power of Prison Yoga* and has published a number of articles on Yoga philosophy.

Reverend Kumari resides with her husband at Yogaville in Buckingham, Virginia.

INDEX